New Sufi Songs and Dances

To dear Karen Sitara
with blessings of
Song & dance

Love, Nirtan
Banff, June 21, 2015

New Sufi Songs and Dances

INSPIRED BY THE WRITINGS OF HAZRAT INAYAT KHAN
including music for the Universal Worship Service

Carol Ann Sokoloff

~ Nirtan ~

Ekstasis Editions

Canadian Cataloguing in Publication Data

Sokoloff, Carol Ann
    New Sufi Songs and Dances.

    ISBN 1-896860-75-3

        1. Sufi music—India—History and criticism.
    2. Dance—Religious aspects—Sufism.   I. Title.
    ML3197.S683   2000   782.3'71   C00-910930-7

For information regarding Sufism please contact:
The International Sufi Movement, 78 Anna Paulownastraat, 2518 BJ
The Hague, Netherlands.

Published in 2000 by:
Ekstasis Editions Canada Ltd.   Ekstasis Editions
Box 8474, Main Postal Outlet   Box 571
Victoria, B.C. V8W 3S1   Banff, Alberta ToL oCo

THE CANADA COUNCIL | LE CONSEIL DES ARTS
FOR THE ARTS | DU CANADA
SINCE 1957 | DEPUIS 1957

New Sufi Songs and Dances has been published with the assistance of a grant from the
Canada Council and the Cultural Services Branch of British Columbia.

To my beloved partner in the dance,
poet Shams Richard Olafson,
for loving support, encouragement,
vision and wisdom.

CONTENTS

Preface: Invitation to the Dance by Hidayat Inayat-Khan   9
Introduction   11
Hazrat Inayat Khan, Poet, Mystic, Musician   21
Why Dance?   18
Reflections on Dance by Hazrat Pir-o-Murshid Inayat Khan   27
Some General Instructions   33
Music, Song and the Voice   35

Part One — Songs & Dances based on Sufi Prayers & Affirmations 37
Toward the One (Invocation)   40
Most Merciful and Compassionate God (Prayer 'Saum')   44
Love, Harmony and Beauty   47
Healing Prayer (Nayaz)   50
I Come From a Perfect Source (Healing Affirmation)   54
Ishq' Allah Mabud L'illah   57
Open Our Hearts (from Prayer 'Khatum')   61
Allah Hu (Zikar Dance)   64
Instructions for Informal Sufi Whirling   66
Bismillah, Ya Rahman Er Rahim   68
Bismillah Greeting   70

Part Two — Songs and Dances from the Nature Meditations   75
Awake My Soul to the Call   78
It is Thou Whom I See   81
I See Thy Beloved Beauty   84
Let Me Become Thy Body   87
Let Every Movement of Life   90

Part Three — Related Heart Songs & Dances   93
Peace is the Longing of Every Soul   97
Song of Trees   100
At One With the Essence of All   103
Oh the Beauty, Oh the Wonder   106
Chanuka, Chanuka   109
Next Year in Jerusalem (Passover Dance)   112

Part Four — A Musical Universal Worship   115
Invocation (Procession)   119
To the Glory   121
We Offer   124
Prayer, Khatum   126

PREFACE

INVITATION TO THE DANCE

by Hidayat Inayat-Khan,
International Sufi Movement

The Soul expresses its inexhaustible energy in so many ways, all of which are characteristic of its celestial relationship with the feeling heart as well as with the thinking world and the physical attunement of one's personality to the Divine within.

This explains why some sing; others dance; others write poems; others paint, carve or mould; and others play or create music. These various types of expressions of the call of the Soul originate either from an ever-flowing source of inspiration, or from coordinated thinking, or perhaps from impressions received.

The Dances and Musical creation of Nirtan Sokoloff, as experienced at Lake O'Hara Sufi Camp and in so many other privileged seminars have the magic power of stimulating graceful movements, besides motivating the fire energy of the heart and attuning the spirit to a level of mystical experiences of purest kind.

May this precious "Invitation to the Dance", or Sufi Song Book offer guidance to the reader and inspiration to the candidate-dancer, whose steps shall lead body, mind and heart to the gate beyond which the Divine is unexpectedly discovered from within.

Hidayat Inayat-Khan
International Sufi Movement

Aziza and Hidayat Inayat-Khan,
Pir-o-Murshid of the Sufi Movement
At launch for the book "The Inner School" at the Rocky Mountain Sufi Camp, Lake O'Hara, June 1997.

INTRODUCTION

In the guise of songs and dances this book chronicles the spiritual adventure which the study of Sufism has been to me. From the four-year-old who whirled about the living room when others were asleep, to the just-six child at summer camp comprehending mystical messages in nature, to the pre-teen who devoured the Rubaiyat of Omar Khayyam, always wondering about that strange quatrain, "Let the Sufi flout," to the nice Jewish girl with an unacceptable fondness for Jesus and all traditions of worship, at every age this path was waiting for me to find it. And eventually, through literature, I came to know the name attached to that philosophy I naturally held. Studying Chaucer in university I became fascinated with some of the deep concepts his entertaining writing disguised. And after university, when finally free to read as I chose, I spent a year devouring the novels of Doris Lessing. In one of them I became interested in the quotes she had used throughout, from Idries Shah's *The Way of the Sufi*. And then one day, while working on a publishing project, a co-worker announced she hoped to take time off to go to a Sufi camp. "What is it?" I asked, and mentioned these quotes. She replied that it had something to do with whirling dervishes, another term with which I was quite unfamiliar. After struggling a little more, my friend suggested that she would invite me to a workshop to find out.

In the meantime I bought *The Way of the Sufi* and found it deeply meaningful. But Sufism remained abstract until my first experience of what was then known as Sufi Dancing (also called Dances of Universal Peace). Led by Shaikh Shahabuddin David Less, in a beautiful old church in downtown Toronto, the impression of recovering a buried part of my being was immediate. Turning in the child-like dance, surrounded by brilliant stained-glass windows and the vaulted arches of the church, I felt ecstasy and the sensation of returning to a state of innocence. From Shahabuddin I learned about his teacher, Murshid Sam (Samuel Lewis, Sufi Ahmed Murad) who had created this form of dancing. I later bought the book *In the Garden* about his life and work.

As my interest in Sufism grew, I attended the first Canadian Sufi camps (in Ontario), and naturally experienced many other aspects of

Sufi practice beyond that of circle dancing. However, as someone who had sung and danced from a very early age, who loved music and wrote poetry, of course this element of not only music, but also dance and poetry involved in a spiritual discipline, would always have a tremendous appeal. Later I delved into a more Islamic-oriented Sufi tradition, whirling and belly-dancing with Iraqi Mevlevi dervish Adnan Sarhan. But then came another Sufi summer camp, and this time I had the good fortune to meet Murshid Shamcher Bryn Beorse.

Shamcher had been one of Inayat Khan's original students (or *mureed* in Sufi terms) back in the 1920's. It was he who explained to me the unique Sufi Message which it had been this Indian musical and Sufi master's mission to give to the world. Almost without words, Shamcher led me to an inner understanding of the nature and being of this great Sufi. From that moment, I no longer felt the need to find a 'more authentic' form of Sufism, realizing that this contemporary ecumenical Sufi Message of Spiritual Liberty, contained in itself the essence of ancient Sufi thought as well as an uplifting, unifying devotional philosophy for today, free of any dogma of organized religion.

It was destiny that soon took me to California, where my father was ill and where Shamcher had moved. Members of the Sufi Islamia Ruhaniat Society were kind enough to put me up at the Khankah in San Francisco's Mission District. How inspiring to attend classes at the home of Samuel Lewis, to drink coffee in his kitchen, to meditate in his garden. Later that year, I lived at the Three Rings House in San Francisco, dedicated to harmony and understanding between Christians, Moslems and Jews and peace in the Middle East. It was work started by Samuel Lewis who felt that if people could eat together, pray together and dance together, there is bound to be peace. I began to understand why Sam had called this dance form he had created 'the Dances of Universal Peace.' While staying at that house, indeed, the signing of the first peace agreement between Israel and Egypt took place, an inspiring event which gave rise to a song and the beginnings of a dance (one I only completed very recently). I remember at that time, I felt that I was somehow working with Murshid Sam on material for that occasion, though nothing came of it for years.

I toyed with the idea of staying in the Bay area and working with Shamcher on his alternative energy initiatives (the promising and still untried OTEC technology), however being Canadian (albeit half-

American) the call to return to Canada is one I have always heeded, no matter where I travelled. Shamcher came up for another Canadian Sufi camp, and he suggested that starting the following year the camps could alternate between Eastern and Western Canada. A group of Sufis in contact with Shamcher's student Carol Sill (Sufia), who lived in Edmonton, Alberta at the time, began arranging locations for the next summer's camp. Miraculously, the Lake O'Hara Lodge location was arranged and the first Rocky Mountain Sufi Camp organized. Unfortunately, merely weeks before that camp, which had been suggested and inspired by Murshid Shamcher Beorse, we learned that his health was failing.

I was among a few Canadians who arrived in Berkeley in time to spend a cheerful morning with this dear friend. He joked with us in his simple apartment, stretched out on a couch, but in such very good spirits it was hard to believe he was as unwell as we had been told. We asked him all sorts of questions, and the conversation came around to the writings of Hazrat Inayat Khan. Shamcher explained the process by which *The Message Volumes* had been created, and that much of Hazrat Inayat Khan's teachings had been taken down by secretaries during lectures, thus having passed through the filter of another's personality. Then Shamcher quoted the third of the Ten Sufi Thoughts, "There is one holy book, the sacred manuscript of nature, the only scripture which can enlighten the reader." Those were, more or less, his parting words, for soon after we all filed out while his daughter Daphne brought him lunch. When we returned after lunch, our friend and teacher, while still breathing, had clearly left his body. It was a strange experience, to be there then, no one really knowing what to do. We simply sat in silence for some time. Closing my eyes, I inwardly perceived the presence of a figure dressed in brown robes, arriving to greet and assist Shamcher in his transition to a new life.

Scarcely had I returned from that journey, when the wonderful Western Canadian Sufis insisted I take part in the first Rocky Mountain camp, even providing my air ticket so as to make it possible. In many ways, I have never recovered from the impression the magnificent Lake O'Hara setting made upon me. As someone who had always loved mountains, to be in the most majestic Alpine splendour of this unspoiled wilderness on the Great Continental Divide, produced a state of ecstasy which I have never gotten over. Although

Shamcher could not be present at the camp as planned, his appreciation for that 'sacred manuscript of nature' so perfectly presented in that place, made one feel he was as present as ever. In his absence Shahabuddin Less established a deep Sufi vibration for the first of what would turn out to be two decades (and still more we hope) of camps. Still, the passing of this inspiring guide had left me convinced there would never again be anyone in my life with whom I could share such a deep and pleasurable Sufi connection.

The following spring I had the opportunity to travel in Israel and Europe. Coincidentally, I shared a connecting flight to Israel with Pir Vilayat Inayat Khan, the son of Shamcher's teacher Inayat Khan. He was leaving Jerusalem as I was arriving and I greatly appreciated his reflections on sites of mystical interest. In Jerusalem I sensed the ancient vibrations and the spiritual geography which is forged into the Judeo-Christian psyche. I learned first-hand of the complexities of relations between Arabs, Christians and Jews and how difficult the process of peace was amongst those who shared much in common and yet were separated by their cultures.

Flying from Jerusalem to Paris, I felt as if these cities were surely on different planets. Since first visiting as a young teen, I have always felt irresistibly drawn to Paris, and I was delighted to return to that most civilized of cities, after the dusty Middle-East. But this time I had a special mission in my heart, to visit Fazal Manzil, the home of Hazrat Inayat Khan, in Suresnes on the outskirts of Paris. Amazingly enough, a telephone number for the home had been published in a book I had carried on my journey. I plucked up my courage and phoned the number, only to be told it was quite impossible to visit as it was a private home. After much begging and pleading on my part, I was referred to someone who could perhaps help me. And so it was that I was able to realize this dream of visiting this place which somehow felt to be my spiritual home.

On that first visit, and on the ones since, I have found that there have been difficulties to overcome in getting to Fazal Manzil. On my first visit, I found myself laughing about something as I began to descend a staircase from a train platform. Before I knew it, I was hurtling down a long set of concrete stairs at a terrible pace, and I wondered what condition I would find myself in when I finally stopped rolling. Miraculously, I was only slightly bruised, although my raincoat was a muddy mess. And so it was a rather dishevelled and completely shaken person who finally arrived at that green oasis in the grey of Paris, which is the garden of Inayat, at Suresnes. However, none of that mattered. I met the person I had spoken to over the phone, and while I was not able to enter the house, I was very pleased to be able simply to linger in the garden for a time.

I found a little bench among some shrubs close to the property line, where I could sit unobtrusively, and there I meditated a short while. Oh, what a feeling came over me. Yes, certainly peace of the Master's presence, but also another tone was unmistakable, that of heartbreak. My impression was that Pir-o-Murshid Inayat Khan despaired at the splintering which had taken place amongst his followers, so contrary to the essence of his message of harmony. "Get close to the family," came an inward voice, although I scarcely understood its meaning.

I left Europe to return to the second Lake O'Hara camp, for despite my love of European travel, the wonders of O'Hara were still more irresistible. Soon after that camp, I moved to Western Canada, (to Banff, Alberta) for what I thought would be a year, but has turned out to be ongoing (later settling in Victoria, on Vancouver Island). A few of the Alberta Sufis had been in contact with the other son of Hazrat Inayat Khan, Pir Hidayat, and had invited him to the forthcoming Rocky Mountain camp. I had heard about Hidayat from Shamcher and had also written to him, as a gesture in response to that inward message I had received at Suresnes. Of course, I looked forward to his planned attendance at the camp. Then problems, or 'challenges' as Shamcher would say, began to manifest.

First Shahabuddin informed us that he could not attend the first part of the camp. Then Pir Hidayat sent regrets that he would not be able to come after all. It seemed like the O'Hara camp was about to fall apart. I suggested that we beg Hidayat to reconsider his position, and so a few of us sent off letters of that nature. I don't know what came over me, but mine was particularly forceful, and after mailing it I was rather alarmed that the recipient might take offense. Naturally, I was delighted when Hidayat agreed to come after all. He apparently asked with some interest about who Wadood (my previous Sufi name) might be.

So it was on a June day in 1982 that Pir Zade Hidayat Inayat-Khan (now Pir-o-Murshid of the Sufi Movement) arrived in Banff, and I received a call inviting me to come meet him. He got on to the phone and said, "It was your letter that made me come." We chatted a little and I found myself laughing at his wonderful sense of humour. I had not encountered such a sense of humour since being in the company of Shamcher. I immediately recognized that feeling of having a very good friend, which in my experience the truest Sufis bring. When I met Pir Hidayat, later that afternoon, I kept feeling, "There is something so familiar about him," but not really able to place it. As anyone who has met both sons of Pir-o-Murshid Inayat Khan can attest, they are on the outside, completely different — so that was not it. Finally, I understood, it was his father Hazrat Inayat Khan, whom Hidayat so reminded me of. Even though I had never met the Sufi Master in the body, still when I met his son Hidayat, I recognized in him the atmosphere of Pir-o-Murshid Inayat Khan with which I had grown thankfully familiar.

That Rocky Mountain Sufi camp was different from any other Sufi gathering I had attended. Pir Hidayat had a distinctive European style and was single-mindedly devoted to his father's Sufi Message and way of performing Sufi practices. He introduced us to the singing Zikar of Hazrat Inayat Khan, which I had known of, but never in the reverent ceremony he presented, with a strict observance of rhythm, tone and body movement. Shahabuddin Less eventually joined the camp for the last few days and one could note how the Sufi Message adapts to the different personalities who carry it — each offering quite different aspects, despite which the Message is able to encompass all.

Later that summer, the centenary of the birth of Hazrat Pir-o-Murshid Inayat Khan was to be celebrated with a gathering at Fazal Manzil, his home outside of Paris, which I had had the good fortune to visit the previous year. After that experience and after meeting Pir Hidayat, I was feeling very drawn to take part in that celebration. At the spur of the moment I booked a ticket and soon found myself negotiating the Paris Metro with very poor high school French, somehow arriving at Suresnes. It had kindly been arranged for me to stay at a little garden house beside Fazal Manzil, and I always cherish the memory of those precious days. It was during that visit that I started a long poem on the life of Noorunnisa Inayat Khan, titled *A Light Unbroken*. (Ekstasis Editions, 1986)

Having followed my inspiration to be in the mountains, I continued to live in Banff for some years. We were blessed to have Pir Hidayat (and also for some years Murshida Hayat, an American original student of Hazrat Inayat Khan, and then eventually Pir Hidayat's wife Murshida Aziza as well) continue to join us for the Rocky Mountain Sufi camp and introduce many of those practices which had been given by his father. One in particular that bears mentioning in the context of this book is that of Rhythmic Walking.

I was familiar with the spiritual walks developed by Samuel Lewis, but I hadn't known that Pir-o-Murshid Inayat Khan had previously suggested a similar walking practice. Pir Hidayat shared with us a training that his father had insisted upon for the children, that of rhythmic walking, in rhythms of three, four, five, six and seven beats, with accents based on the Indian *talas* or rhythms. Naturally to both Hazrat Inayat Khan, a master of Indian music, and to his son Hidayat, a composer of modern symphonic music, the concept of rhythm was of the greatest importance. Pir Hidayat showed us steps to use in these rhythmic walks, and suggested *wazifas* (or sacred names) to accompany them, to aid in keeping the rhythms and the accents consistent. Later these were tied to the elements (earth, water, fire, air, ether) and eventually incorporated in a Ziraat ceremony, or celebration of the elements, another of his father's rituals.

I mention these walks because they are not far removed from the practice of spiritual dance. It is to Samuel Lewis that we owe the formulation of this way of joining together in contemplative dance that is now known as the 'Dances of Universal Peace.' Murshid Sam had been inspired by the modern dancer Ruth St. Denis, a friend and associate. She too was influenced by Hazrat Inayat Khan, who served as her musician during his initial years in the West. It was Ruth St. Denis who dreamed of dance as worship, and longed to bring to the world a celebration of Holy Mass which would be danced. Samuel Lewis, one of the youngest of Hazrat Inayat Khan's original students, later received training in Islamic Sufism, Zen Buddhism, and Hinduism as well as his own Jewish heritage, complete with Israeli-type folk-dancing. In the late 1960's, he was able to put all these streams together to create a drug-free route to ecstatic experience for the flower-children who had converged in his native San Francisco. His dances combined dervish whirling (the traditional Sufi dance), Hazrat Inayat Khan's rhythmic walks, Ruth St. Denis' devotional attitude to dance, the joyous coming together of folk dance circles, and sacred phrases from world traditions. This was a potent mixture which immediately and to this day is a most magnetic and attractive introduction to spiritual life.

During one Lake O'Hara Sufi camp, I asked Pir Hidayat, for a new Sufi name. He suggested a few for me to choose, but I left the choice to him. And so I took the name 'Nirtan,' the name of one of Hazrat Inayat Khan's books of aphorisms, meaning 'the dance of the soul,' from the Hindu term *nirtya*, meaning dance. Many wonder about the purpose or effect of taking on a spiritual name, and it is explained that not only one's self, but also one's community, benefit from the vibrations carried by the name. In my own case, this name coincided with a process of returning to 'dance' as a central focus in my life, although it is only in retrospect that I have understood this. While I had studied ballet, modern and jazz dance from childhood onward, and had initially been attracted to the dance aspect of the Sufi practices, there was a period during which my interest in dance had fallen away. Gradually, perhaps as a result of taking the name 'Nirtan' a reawakening to dance unfolded.

By 1986 I had married Shams Richard Olafson (at Lake O'Hara camp) and moved to Victoria, BC and given birth to our eldest son. Wishing to restore my physical condition after childbirth, I enrolled in a belly dancing class, for of all the dance arts I had studied, I considered middle-eastern dance to be the most natural and spiritual. Soon I became part of a performing group, and by the time I was pregnant with our younger son, I was teaching pre-natal belly dance. I do consider belly-dancing to be a spiritual dance, a true mind/body/heart discipline which becomes an exploration of feminine energy, a healing journey of mastery and empowerment. This is a most misunderstood art form, which again through dancer Ruth St. Denis (an orientalist and teacher of Martha Graham) has had a profound impact on contemporary dance. Only recently has there been some long overdue public recognition of middle-eastern ethnic dance as an art.

During my first few years in Victoria, there were only two or three Sufi friends in residence. We would attempt to get together for dancing, which I again found enjoyable after a period of being mainly interested in dervish whirling. One winter, my infant child was ill, and I found myself nursing him with a musical version of the Healing

18

Prayer, Nayaz. I had composed a musical setting for this prayer years before, but had found it's melody overly melancholic for such an affirmative healing meditation, so I reworked that original composition to make it more rhythmic, creating a chorus of the final line of the prayer. As I walked around my child's cradle, singing that chorus, I began to visualize the movements of a dance. Later I shared these ideas with my few Sufi friends, and they suggested some improvements. In this way, the Healing Prayer dance was born and carried to various gatherings where it received a very positive response. After that, other songs and dances started coming to me and I would try them out on whomever was available. Some came together at the O'Hara camp, where the encouragement of the participants inspired me to keep working in this way. Others emerged from dance meetings which I had now begun to hold monthly in Victoria, BC. Similarly the support and encouragement of our Victoria Sufi community, and their willingness to experiment with and collaborate on new and untested dances, has made it possible for the dances in this book to be presented.

To all these people — Basira, Bob, Sharda, Akbar, Ameena, Ameen, Sufia, Kuan Yin, Willo, Jelaluddin, Alix and Robert, Zohra, and Amir (to name but a few) and the many, many others who have participated in the creation of dances over the years, I offer my deepest gratitude and appreciation for the invaluable role you have played. A few special friends have also made this book possible and they are Hakima Boyce (for prodding), Bhakti Moore (for proofing), music copyist Blaine Dunaway and my beloved husband Shams Richard, dreamer and dream-maker.

To our most inspiring teacher Pir-o-Murshid Hidayat Inayat Khan, who overcame an initial hesitancy regarding this dance as Sufi practice to offer me great encouragement to create new dances and the opportunity to lead dancing at the O'Hara camp, and to Murshida Aziza, a shining example of Sufi dedication and an enthusiastic participant in our dance circles at the camp, I am hard pressed to express in words the depth of my gratitude and indebtedness. And finally, to Hazrat Pir-o-Murshid Inayat Khan, whose uplifting and poetic words have provided the lyrical inspiration for most of the songs on which these dances are based, I bow in deepest devotion to the tremendous contribution he has made to the lives of mureeds and to the enlightening of humanity.

It is only in the writing of this book, that I realize that Pir-o-Murshid Inayat Khan, whose living presence is tangible to those who seek it, has been, as it were, my primary songwriting collaborator in these songs and dances. This is not surprising as he has said, "My work I give unto your hands," and indeed all those who are working for this Message of Spiritual Liberty are also the collaborators of Hazrat Inayat Khan. I chose to call our local dance meeting 'Sufi Dancing' because as the Sufi Movement representative in Victoria, British Columbia my interest in dancing was inextricably linked with the Sufi path. Besides, while we of course, share the Dances of Universal Peace so beloved in dance circles, the original dances I was creating were almost entirely based on the Sufi prayers, aphorisms and practices of Hazrat Inayat Khan.

Each meeting begins with a speaking and then a chanting of the Sufi Invocation 'Toward the One.' Pir Hidayat once mentioned that during his father's time this Invocation had been sung on a single tone, the final line fading away as the 'Spirit of Guidance' is invoked. I have clung to this practice, which I find a most wonderful way of attuning to each other, to harmony of purpose, to a rhythmic regulation of the breath and a warming up of the vocal chords.

Over the years, people from elsewhere attending O'Hara camp (now in its twenty-first year) have asked for tapes and dance instructions in order to be able to take the dances home with them to their own circles. This book has been long in the making, but once started has been fairly swift in the coming together. To all these people, and others who may eventually wish to lead or share these Inayat Khan Sufi songs and dances, I offer my hopes that you will find this material to be useful and the songs and dances enjoyable.

Music and dance are living arts, and while fidelity to the spirit and lyrics and melody will insure some kind of consistency, I would encourage those who wish to improvise or expand upon suggested movements to feel free to do so. Do make these dances your own. Find the way in which it is appropriate for your circle to perform them, or a way in which an individual may use these songs for personal spiritual practice combining mantra, movement and music. I will be very grateful to learn of any experience with these songs and dances, that any reader would be inclined to share. May the Spirit of Guidance guide our dancing path. Happy singing, happy dancing on this blessed Sufi trail....

Nirtan (Carol Ann Sokoloff) Victoria, BC.
September, 2000

HAZRAT INAYAT KHAN,
POET, MYSTIC, MUSICIAN

My soul is moved to dance
  by the charm of Thy graceful movements,
And my heart beateth the rhythm
  of Thy gentle steps.
The sweet impression
  of Thy winning countenance,
  my worshipped One,
covereth all visible things from my sight.
My heart re-echoes the melody
  Thou playest on Thy flute.
And it bringeth my soul in harmony
  with the whole universe.

  Hazrat Inayat Khan, Gayan

NEW SUFI SONGS AND DANCES

Most of the songs and dances in this collection have been inspired by the writings of Hazrat Pir-o-Murshid Inayat Khan (1882-1927), the noted Indian musical and Sufi master who brought both Indian music and Sufi spiritual teachings to the Western world in 1910. From an illustrious family of Indian musicians, Hazrat Inayat Khan was considered one of India's greatest singers and Veena players. He was greatly attracted to mysticism and became a student of Sufism under the guidance of Murshid Sayyed Abu Hashim Madani of the Chistia order. From his Murshid, the young Inayat received a blessing to travel to the west to introduce Sufi spiritual teachings and to unite East and West through music.

From the years 1910 to 1927, Inayat Khan (honoured as Hazrat after his passing) travelled in Europe and America, giving concerts and lectures, and eventually organizing the Sufi Movement and its esoteric school, the Sufi Order. His message of Spiritual Liberty was integral to the esoteric work he introduced, accommodating those of all religious faiths and emphasizing a non-dogmatic, ecumenical approach to mysticism. This was a new, contemporary Sufi thought, a response to the needs of the time and cultures, but rooted in the ancient traditions of the Sufis of the East. Inayat Khan married a young American, Ora Ray Baker (Amina Begum), and their four children, Vilayat (leader of the Sufi Order in the West), Hidayat (leader of the Sufi Movement), Noorunnisa (the WWII martyr 'Madeleine') and Khairunnisa have been a tremendous influence in the continuance of their father's message. In addition, the many students to whom Hazrat Inayat Khan was a beloved spiritual guide, became the spiritual guides for the seekers of yesterday and today, and their students are continuing to carry this same Message. It is to this Spirit of Guidance which has assisted so many in the journey of the soul that this book is also humbly offered.

Why Dance?

In my experience, people are drawn to these spiritual circle dances for many reasons. Some take part for purely social reasons, others for a love of music and movement, some out of interest in Sufism, or curiosity about this form of 'moving meditation.' Others come as a commitment to peace amongst differing cultures and traditions, and some feel drawn by the child-like joy of the simple dances, the feeling of love and light and peace one attains through this practice. And many find themselves drawn to return again and again, for no reason whatsoever, except that their soul is somehow satisfied by this spiritual food for which it has hungered. It matters little why people are attracted to these sacred dances, for it is far more interesting to consider that which takes place through the dance.

I am always amazed at the transformative power of this practice, which I have observed again and again. A regular dance meeting is held or a special dance occasion organized — one arrives and the room fills up with people. Most of them are strangers to this practice and to each other. One can sense their uncertainty — why are they there, what are they to expect? People keep their distance, their reserve and politely study any literature on the table, or occasionally engage in conversation with someone nearby. Then we join together to form a circle or start a walking circle in which we allow our bodies to move freely and come into a given rhythm. Standing in place, holding hands in the circle, we breathe together deeply, taking the opportunity each breath presents to exhale impurities and stale conditions and thoughts, and to inhale pure, life-giving *prana* or spirit. We draw our attention to our feet and our connection with the earth element rising from the soles of feet through our bodies; and to our head which draws heavenly etheric energy down through our bodies. We imagine these energies meeting in that centre of our being which Sufis call the heart, and we feel that heart illuminated by consciousness and breath, becoming a luminous centre whose light radiates down our arms and through our joined palms and fingertips, our circle electrified in a vibratory current, becoming a luminous circle. When we feel attuned as a circle, united in harmony and illuminated by the radiant current of consciousness, we begin by speaking and then singing the Sufi Invocation. Usually, this is so deeply attuned, so wonderfully harmonious that even without anything more being done, a magical transformation is already underway. Then we start to dance. Instruments need to be tuned, and in doing so, the musicians and dance leader tune themselves. The instructions for the dance are explained, and in the process the ice is further broken as we try out melodies and movements. While the atmosphere is devotional, there is still room to share laughter, which helps put everyone at ease. When we finally start the dance, it is joy that dances in the room. Now the transformations intensify.

Through singing a melody an entire circle of people are naturally breathing in a given rhythm. Voices join together in harmony and by keeping the circle round the capacity for harmony grows. The heart beats fully and dancers experience the upliftment of conscious movement — creating a desired thought-form of peace or love, through infusing movement with Divine awareness. Dance has been described as 'intentional movement,' and in this case the intention is nothing less than identification with a Divine Ideal. The meaning of the words sung and the potent vibrations of the sacred syllables intoned create an atmosphere which reverberates both within each dancer and from the circle as a whole. So many faculties are exercised at once — rhythm, breath, tone, harmony, conscious movement, potent sounds — the brain is so fully occupied it can no longer hold onto its usual patterns. One simply forgets one's self, lost in the magic of the dance. As Pir Hidayat Inayat-Khan says of the *zikar*, "The mask of the ego is dropped"; for when that ever-present ego identification is allowed to fall away, the essential Divine nature or soul energy, the true ego, has room for expression. It is this phenomenon which is referred to by the poet W.B. Yeats in his question, "How can we know the dancer from the dance?" As the ego-level personalities of the individuals recede, the Divine soul force of the dance builds. Whichever Divine attribute is affirmed through the dance begins to manifest. Any confusions or difficulties which threatened to disrupt the dance, generally are resolved without intervention as that higher mind which is the Spirit of Guidance is able to guide and direct. Joy, peace, ecstasy are experienced as bodies, hearts and souls move together in harmony, sending harmonious vibrations outward in ever-expanding circles of influence.

After each dance, rather than expressing this joy, a brief silence is maintained, as the energy created is drawn inward, to hear the voice of the heart from within. It is understood that in many ways the dance itself is simply a preparation for the mystical silence experienced when the dancing and singing stops. Thus with every dance the atmosphere deepens and the intensity and attunement increases. During partner dances, individuals greet, not only on the level of personality but on the deep soul level, recognizing and reflecting Divinity within. Again and again we give and receive, give and receive...emptying ourselves of our selves in order to receive divine energy, love and light. By the end of the session, the total strangers of a few hours before, have shared a deeply meaningful experience, have seen the Divine shining through each other's eyes and have had their own divine nature reflected back to them, have become friends on the deep soul level of fellow-travellers on the spiritual journey, and are embracing in warm Sufi hugs which honour the nobility of the soul. The atmosphere is charged with love, harmony, and beauty and long after the last dance is shared, the closing prayer recited, that feeling of peace — peace within and peace without, prevails.

O chestnut tree, great rooted blossomer,
Are you the leaf, the blossom or the bole?
O body swayed to music, O brightening glance,
How can we know the dancer from the dance?
W.B. Yeats, "Among School Children"

Reflections on Dance
from the writings of Hazrat Inayat Khan

The use of music and movement as spiritual practice, as employed by Murshid Samuel Lewis in the creation of his Dances of Universal Peace, is frequently referred to in the teachings of Hazrat Pir-o-Murshid Inayat Khan (1882-1927), the Indian mystic and musician who brought the Sufi Message of Spiritual Liberty to the western world and the source of many Sufi organizations operating today, including the Sufi Movement, the Sufi Order and the Sufi Islamia Ruhaniat Society. The following passages from the The Sufi Message Volumes are a sampling of the Master's teachings on these related subjects. They have been edited slightly in order to present in this abbreviated form and also for the purpose of gender-inclusivity. The quotations are taken from the revised editions published in Holland by Servire BV, 1979.

From *The Mysticism of Sound (Vol.II):*

If vibratory activity is properly controlled, one may experience all life's joy, and at the same time not be enslaved by it...The saints and sages spread their peace...in accordance with the power of the vibrations they send out from their soul. (p. 20)

If a Sufi sends forth vibrations of thought and feeling, they naturally strike with a great strength and power on any mind on which they happen to fall. As sweetness of voice has a winning power, so it is with tenderness of thought and feeling. Thought-vibrations to which the spoken word is added are doubled in strength; and with a physical effort this strength is trebled. (p. 21)

The Sufi, like a student of music, trains both the voice and the ear in the harmony of life. The training of voice consists in being conscientious about each word spoken, about its tone, rhythm, meaning and the appropriateness for the occasion. For instance the words of consolation should be spoken in a slow rhythm, with a soft voice and sympathetic tone. When speaking words of command a lively rhythm is necessary, and a powerful and distinct voice. The Sufi avoids all unrhythmic actions; keeping the rhythm of speech under the control of patience, not speaking a word before the right time...In order to keep harmony the Sufi even modulates the speech from one key to another...falling in with another person's idea by looking at the subject from the speaker's point of view instead of one's own. The Sufi makes a base for every conversation with an appropriate introduction, thus preparing the ears of the listener for a perfect response. The Sufi watches one's every movement and expression, as well as those of others, trying to form a consonant chord of harmony between oneself and another. (p. 29, 30)

Motion is the significance of life, and the law of motion is rhythm. Rhythm is life disguised in motion...There is a saying in Sanskrit that tone is the mother of nature, but that rhythm is its father...The infant begins life on earth by moving its arms and legs, thus showing the rhythm of its nature, and illustrating the philosophy which teaches that rhythm is the sign of life. The inclination to dance shown by every human illustrates also that innate nature of beauty which chooses rhythm for its expression. (p. 44)

Rhythm produces an ecstasy which is inexplicable and incomparable with any other source of intoxication. This is why the dance has been the most fascinating pastime of all people, both civilized and savage, and has delighted alike, saint and sinner. (p. 44)

In order to become a master musician in India, one must master thoroughly not only *raga*, the scale, but also *tala*, the rhythm. Indians as a race are naturally inclined to rhythm; their dance the *Tandeva Nrutya*, the dance of the South, is an expression of rhythm through movement. In the Hindu science of Music there are five different rhythms which are generally derived from the study of nature...(p. 45)

In the traditions of the Sufis *Raqs*, the sacred dance of spiritual ecstasy which even now is prevalent among the Sufis of the East, is traced to the time when contemplation of the Creator impressed the wonderful reality of the vision of God so deeply on the heart of Jelal-ud-Din Rumi that he became entirely absorbed in the whole and single immanence of nature, and took a rhythmic turn which caused the skirt of his garment to form a circle, and the movements of his hands and neck made a circle; and it is the memory of this moment of vision which is celebrated in the dance of the dervishes. Even in the lower creation, among beasts and birds, their joy is always expressed in dance; a bird like the peacock, when conscious of his beauty and of the beauty of the forest around him, expresses his joy in dance. Dance arouses passion and emotion in all living creatures. (p. 46)

Sufis, in order to awaken in a person that part of our emotional nature which is generally asleep, have a rhythmic practice which sets the whole mechanism of body and mind in rhythm... (p. 46)

The art of music in the east is called *Kala* and has three aspects: vocal, instrumental and expressing movement....after vocal and instrumental music comes the motional music of the dance. Motion is the nature of vibration. Every motion contains within itself a thought and feeling...motion is the sign of life, and when accompanied with music, it sets both performer and onlooker in motion.

The mystics have always looked upon this subject as a sacred art. In the Hebrew scriptures we find David dancing before the Lord; and the gods and goddesses of the Greeks, Egyptians, Buddhists and Brahmins are represented in different poses, all having a certain meaning and philosophy, relating to the great cosmic dance which is evolution.

Even up to the present time among Sufis in the East dancing takes place at their sacred meetings called Suma, for dancing is the outcome of joy. The dervishes at the Suma give an outlet to their ecstasy in *Raqs* which is regarded with great respect and reverence by those present, and is in itself a sacred ceremony. (p. 57)

Tune and rhythm tend to produce an inclination for dance. To sum up, dancing may be said to be a graceful expression of thought and feeling without uttering a word. It may be used also to impress the soul by movement, by producing an ideal picture before it. When beauty of movement is taken as the presentment of the divine ideal, then the dance becomes sacred. (p. 58)

From *Cosmic Language (Vol.II):*

When you ring the bell the action takes only a moment, but the resonance lasts. It lasts to our knowledge only as long as it is audible; and then it passes on further and it is no longer audible to us; but it exists somewhere, it goes on.

If a pebble thrown into the sea puts the water in action, one hardly stops to think to what extent this vibration acts upon the sea. What one can see is the little waves and circles that the pebble produces before one. One sees only these. But the vibration which it has produced in the sea reaches much further than one can ever imagine...Does this not make us responsible for every movement we make, for every thought that we think, for every feeling that passes through our mind and heart? For there is not one moment of our life wasted, if we only know how to utilize our action here, how to direct our thought, how to express it in words, how to further it with our movement, how to feel it, so that it may make its own atmosphere.

From *Philosophy, Psychology, Mysticism (Vol. XI):*

Every movement has a greater significance than one can imagine...a movement, according to its nature and character, can make an impression on the person who sees it or on the one who makes it, an effect which can automatically work to form a destiny in their lives...In the ceremonies and rituals of ancient peoples every movement had a psychological significance.

The blessings given by the sages, the good wishes and prayers of the masters, were always connected with movement. The movements made the prayer alive; they insured that the blessings were granted. No doubt if movement is without silent thought and deep feeling it is less than thought and feeling, it is almost nothing; but when a movement is made with a living and sincere thought, and with deep feeling, it will make the thought and feeling a thousand times more effective.(p. 95)

From *The Smiling Forehead:*

Our souls are only created to dance; it is their nature to dance and it is the tragedy of life when the soul is kept from dancing. Our craving for comfort and outward satisfaction, our ambition, our desires are nothing but the longing to experience that dance as we know it. Paradise is pictured by every teacher as a place where there is music and dance. Music itself is dance, poetry is the dance of words, singing the dance of the voice. Only when inspiration comes naturally it is a life coming from the depth of the individual.

From *Nature Meditations* (Omega Publications,1980, p.65):
On Movements:
Inward movement means strength and control. Outward movement means exhaustion and expulsion. Zigzag movement means strength but destruction. Side movement directed from right to left means strength and power. Side movement directed from left to right means gentleness and modesty. Side movement directed upwards means love and purity. Side movement directed downwards means affection and hunility.

MURSHID SHAMCHER BRYN BEORSE

Some General Instructions for These Dances

The following suggestions reflect my personal approach to leading dances. Further information on this subject is available from Peaceworks International Network for the Dances of Universal Peace (P.O. Box 55994, Seattle, WA,98155, USA www.dancesofuniversalpeace.org)

Start dance meeting with gentle, free walking in a circle; quiet breathing together or guided meditation, holding hands in circle. Focus awareness on the breath and the opportunity each conscious breath provides, to release pollutants or negative thoughts and inhale pure *prana.* Consider the earth connection through the feet, the divine energy of the heavens through the crown of head, both energies meeting in the luminous heart centre and radiating through arms into hands, through hands to fingertips and around the circle, establishing a current of energy and light.

Begin with spoken Invocation, said a few times. Follow by a chanted 'Toward the One' a very beautiful way to establish a fine vibration, softening on the final line 'the Spirit of Guidance.' This is also a good way to gently warm up the vocal chords for singing.

Maintain balance and harmony during dances by keeping the circle round, every person able to see every other person. Try alternating men and women, unless some members are more comfortable otherwise. Hands can be held right palm up, left palm down (as in whirling), so energy travels from hand to heart and out again. Strive to keep all elements in balance, ie. rhythm, harmony, voice, and voices blending harmoniously.

Hands joined: Hands can be joined as described above, or in any fashion that is comfortable. Keep hands joined until instructions indicate releasing hands or for a spin.

Spinning: Traditionally Sufi spinning is done counter-clockwise (to left), with right palm up, left palm down, eyes unfocussed, consciousness centred in heart chakra. (see Allah Hu,Whirling Dance p.64-66).

Partner sequences: Standing in circle, turn to a person next to you to be a partner. This is the direction a dancer will always turn to find their partner when a partner sequence begins, and usually the direction in which dancers will move when progressing to a new partner. In many cases, the next partner to whom one will progress is the person whose eyes one meets, looking past one's partner's shoulder. Do establish eye contact with partner, seeing not their limited personality but the deep soul essence of their being, the Divine Nature which, through your recognition, you allow them to embody. They will also be reflecting your own deep essence and Divine Nature back to you.

End each dance with a short silence, long enough to experience the effect the dance has left. Understand that in many ways, the song and dance are merely a preparation for the awakening available in the moments of stillness and silence afterwards. Resist the urge to express and dissipate energy created through dance. Instead allow energy to be contained within, empowering one and allowing the dance circle to evolve to a deeper level. The silence can be broken with a simple 'Amen' or other appropriate affirmation.

These songs and dances are meant to be living. By all means, allow the inspiration of the moment to infuse them in any way which is appropriate. Do add harmony with the voice and improvise on the movements when desired.

For Musicians: Songs are notated in keys to accommodate most voices. Guitarists can use a capo to raise or lower pitch as required. Chord symbols reflect standard guitar tuning. The capo can also be used to simplify chords played. Check the dance instructions for capo suggestions. Keep rhythm steady at all times and stay attuned to the dance leader.

Recordings by the author of vocal and guitar versions of all songs and dances are available on two CD's from the publisher at the address in the front of this book or at **www.ekstasiseditions.com**.

MUSIC, SONG AND VOICE

The beauty and power of these dances as a spiritual practice derives from their successful combination of the elements of voice (which is made of breath), conscious movement, potent sound (vibration) and concentrated thought on an empowering ideal. It is clear therefore that the vocal and musical aspects play a tremendous role, and when in consonance create the ideal of heavenly harmony.

The voice itself is the manifestation of the breath, that mechanism which connects us to our source. Therefore the singing of the songs for dances, is a most important element, magnetizing the atmosphere with Divine energy or light, in addition to the creation of a consistent rhythm of breath amongst all present. Individually, the breath flows freely through all channels and organs of the body, infusing light and oxygen.

To gently warm up the voice through some preliminary walking, moving and then standing still in the circle for conscious breathing followed by a chanted tone (as suggested for the Invocation), takes only a few minutes.

When the singing begins, let it be natural, unforced, in harmony with the circle in respect to volume and pitch. Some who are unused to public singing may find it difficult to let their voice be heard, and these need to be encouraged to 'sing out.' Others with powerful trained voices may need to be careful to 'hold back' somewhat.

Try to be conscious at all times, and if leading the dances, to help the dancers be conscious, that the breath has a radiance, a light which also dances through the singing of the songs — that the voice itself is a kind of dancing of the breath. To simply say or sing the word 'Allah,' allowing the final syllable to hover and vibrate around the heart is often enough to bring the light and vibratory power of the breath and voice to awareness.

MURSHID SAMUEL L. LEWIS
CREATOR OF THE DANCES OF UNIVERSAL PEACE

Part One

Songs & Dances based on Sufi Prayers & Affirmations

The practices, prayers and affirmations offered by the Sufi mystic Hazrat Pir-o-Murshid Inayat Khan (1882-1927) are an obvious resource for the creation of new Sufi songs and dances. Not only are they of deep, vibratory significance, but also genuinely poetic, lending themselves to musical and kinetic interpretation. Through music, students of Sufism may discover a learning aid in the memorization of these precious texts as well as a way of making greater use of them in daily life. Generally, slight alterations of texts have occurred in the transition from the speaking to the singing voice. Sometimes, as in "Most Merciful and Compassionate God" only a portion of a prayer ('Saum') has been used, with an occasional line omitted. In other instances, such as the "Toward the One" song and dance, the original text is intact with the addition of a line, in this case the chorus, 'Oh, Spirit of Guidance guide my way'. This is also true of "The Healing Prayer" song and dance where the last line of the prayer is repeated as a chorus, with the word 'heal' also repeated for emphasis. In every case it is inspiration which has suggested the ways of using the texts and the melodies to carry them. Therefore the spirit and attunement of each is fully retained and in many ways enhanced through the opportunity to allow the dancing of the voice in song, and the dancing of the body and soul in conscious movement, creating harmony and peace.

TOWARD THE ONE

By C.A. Sokoloff, Words By Inayat Khan

© Copyright 1988

Toward the One

Sufi Invocation

Music by C.A. Sokoloff (Nirtan)   *Words by Hazrat Inayat Khan*

Newcomers to contemporary Sufism can easily learn Hazrat Inayat Khan's remarkable 'Invocation' in the course of performing this dance. The dance is lively and fun and involves a joyful greeting of heart and souls in a grand chain. For this purpose a repeated chorus invoking the presence of the 'Spirit of Guidance' has been added to the Invocation. The attunement of the dance is on actually moving, both physically and spiritually, 'Toward the One,' in the realization that wherever we journey, wherever life takes us, we are always, in fact, moving toward the One Being; that whomever we meet, it is the one Divine Beloved we meet. During the grand chain on the chorus, 'Oh Spirit of Guidance guide my way,' dancers can feel that it is this spirit which is drawing them forward through the outstretched hands of other dancers in the circle. When making eye-contact in this greeting, attune to the Spirit of Guidance reflected in the faces of those one greets. This dance makes a good opening dance for experienced groups of dancers, although it may be overly complex for novices to tackle at the start of a meeting. I generally end the dance by simply allowing the 'Spirit of Guidance' grand chain to continue for several minutes.

TOWARD THE ONE

LYRICS:
1. Toward the One,
2. the perfection of Love,
3. Harmony and Beauty,
4. The Only Being,
5. United with All
6. the Illuminated Souls,
7. who form the embodiment
8. of the Master,
9. the Spirit of Guidance.
10. Oh, Spirit of Guidance, guide my way. (chorus, repeat 4 times)

MOVEMENTS:

Dance starts in a circle, but everyone facing to their right, prepared to walk in a counter-clockwise direction.

1. Walking, raising outstretched arms into the air in front of one, palms upward

2. Continue walking, palms come together above head (on 'perfection') and are lowered to heart (palms still together) on 'Love'

3. Continue walking, hands move up above head opening out on 'harmony', moving downwards, palms down on 'beauty'

4. Facing in to the circle, with a slight step back bring hands together at heart on 'only' and then bowing head in humility on 'being', hands come down to sides

5. joining hands, stepping into the circle, raising arms in front

6. letting go of hands, but keeping arms high, palms to the centre of the circle, stepping backwards, as if being actually forced by a powerful and brilliant illumination

TOWARD THE ONE

7. standing in circle, facing in, take left hand and place it on right shoulder on the word 'form', and take right hand and place it on left shoulder on 'embodiment' (arms are crossed over each other)

8. right hand is lifted from shoulder and into air, palm up (on 'of the'), then left hand is taken from shoulder and descends to left side, palm down (on 'master'). This is the pose of the magus or master from the tarot pack, it is also the position for dervish whirling, right palm up, receiving divine energy, left palm down, releasing it.

9. spinning counter-clockwise (to left)

10. grand chain, turn to partner (previously established); the direction in which you turn is the direction in which you move, stretch out right hand and clasp the right hand of partner, moving forward past partner, stretch out left hand to next person's left hand and repeat. This segment should be done at a relaxed, moderate pace in relation to the rhythm of the chorus — you should greet three or four people during each of the four repetitions of the chorus. On the last repetition, as chorus is ending, greet next partner, but then turn to face the centre of the circle. That person will be your partner on the next chorus.

MOST MERCIFUL AND COMPASSIONATE GOD

By C.A. Sokoloff, Words By Inayat Khan

MOST MERCIFUL AND COMPASSIONATE GOD
From the Sufi Prayer 'Saum'
Music by C.A. Sokoloff (Nirtan)   *Words by Hazrat Inayat Khan*

This is a good dance with which to open a dance meeting, invoking the qualities of Divine Mercy and Compassion, by using the lovely words of the prayer 'Saum'. I find it can be most appropriate for those situations in which a group may not be comfortable with the Arabic 'Bismillah, Er Rahman, Er Rahim' (In the name of Allah, who is Mercy and Compassion) with which dance meetings have often opened. This dance also helps introduce the wonderful Sufi prayers of Hazrat Inayat Khan to those who may be unfamiliar with them. The feeling of the dance is both worshipful and joyous.

Saum
Praise be to Thee, Most Supreme God,
Omnipotent, Omnipresent, All-pervading, the Only Being.
Take us in Thy Parental Arms,
Raise us from the denseness of the earth. Thy Beauty do we worship,
to Thee do we give willing surrender;
Most Merciful and Compassionate God,
The Idealized Lord of the whole humanity,
Thee only do we worship and towards Thee alone
do we aspire. Open our hearts towards Thy Beauty,
Illuminate our souls with Thy Divine Light
O Thou, the Perfection of Love, Harmony and Beauty!
All-powerful Creator, Sustainer, Judge
and Forgiver of our shortcomings, Lord God of the East
and of the West, of the worlds above and below
and of the seen and unseen beings,
Pour upon us Thy Love and Thy Light,
Give sustenance to our bodies, hearts and souls,
Use us for the purpose that Thy Wisdom chooseth,
And guide us on the path of Thine Own Goodness.
Draw us closer to Thee every moment of our life,
Until in us be reflected Thy Grace, Thy Glory, Thy Wisdom,
Thy Joy and Thy Peace.   *Amen.*

MOST MERCIFUL AND COMPASSIONATE GOD

LYRICS:
1. Most Merciful and Compassionate God
2. Thee only do we worship. (Repeat 1 & 2)
3. And Toward Thee Alone do we aspire.
4. Open our hearts toward Thy Beauty,
5. Illuminate our souls with Thy Divine Light.
(repeat 4 & 5, two or three times)

MOVEMENTS:
1. Holding hands in a circle rhythmically take 8 small steps into circle raising arms and eyes heavenward,

2. take 8 small steps backwards, bowing in worship (repeat 1 & 2)

3. walking to the right, raise arms on 'do we aspire'

4. Let go of hands. Starting with hands on heart, open arms and hands out, palms up, greeting all directions

5. spin to left, right palm up, left palm down, centred in heart (repeat 4 & 5 two or three times, on the third time, opening of heart movement can be done in toward the centre of the circle).

After a few repetitions, the chorus (nos. 4 & 5) can be done while walking about freely greeting different members of the circle, returning to directions for 1.

Love, Harmony & Beauty
(Sufi Ideals)
Words & Music by C.A.Sokoloff (Nirtan)

Hazrat Pir-o-Murshid Inayat Khan frequently described Sufism as 'a religious philosophy of Love, Harmony and Beauty.' I remember at a Lake O'Hara Sufi camp his son Pir Hidayat Inayat-Khan stating that it is very simple to know what to do and what not to do in life if one only keeps in mind these three Sufi ideals. "Ask yourself," Pir Hidayat suggested, when considering actions, "is it Love; is it Harmony; is it Beauty?" Very soon after that guidance, this dance came into being, and has been a great favourite at the O'Hara camp ever since. This is a joyous, rhythmic celebratory dance which creates an infectious spell of Love, Harmony and Beauty. By simply repeating these words, one partakes of their blessing. A chorus of the repetition of the Arabic name of God, Allah, meaning the One, offers an opportunity to revolve with revolving partners, receiving a deep transmission through each.

How the words 'love', 'harmony', and 'beauty' delight the heart of everyone who hears them!...Love is the nature of life, beauty is the outcome of life, harmony is the means by which life accomplishes its purpose, and the lack of it results in destruction...When we reflect upon this whole creation we cannot but see that its purpose is to express an ideal of love, harmony and beauty...God is love and has created humanity out of love...love is the only power that has created or can create...Love is greater than beauty, because love is the creator of the beauty that love loves in its life...
Hazrat Inayat Khan, In An Eastern Rose Garden

Love creates beauty by her own hands, to worship.

Love develops into harmony,
and of harmony is born of beauty.

Beauty is the life of the artist, the soul of the poet and the theme of the musician.
Hazrat Inayat Khan, Gayan, Vadan, Nirtan

LOVE, HARMONY, AND BEAUTY

By C.A.Sokoloff

© Copyright 1988

Note: The partner part of this dance can be more difficult to explain than to do. Ask dancers to relax and enjoy the dance and not worry too much about the details but let the higher mind direct. Be sure to always progress past the fourth and final partner and greet the person who will be the partner on the next chorus, but then turn into to circle. To end dance let the 'Allah' chorus and the revolving partner rotations continue as long as appropriate. The rhythmic turning involved in this part of the dance does produce a kind of ecstatic trance, but can become dizzying for some, so leaders should be sensitive to the length of time it continues.

LOVE, HARMONY AND BEAUTY

LYRICS:
1. Love, love, love
2. Harmony
3. and Beauty
(repeat 1, 2, 3 a total of three times)
4. Allah, Allah, Allah, Allah,
   Allah, Allah, Allah, Allah

MOVEMENTS:
1. Start in circle, facing in a line of direction, probably to the right. While walking in this direction, the action for the singing of 'Love, love, love' is taken from a traditional middle-eastern folkloric dance step known as 'seed-sowing'. In this case we are sowing little seeds of love, all over the ground on which we walk. We start with our right hand at the heart, and with palm up, we open the arm outwards, scattering seeds of love.We then repeat with the left hand, and again with the right (ie. arms and steps Right, Left, Right on 'Love, love, love')

2. still walking, palms come together at heart and hands rise up and open out above head

3. hands continue in an arc, moving down to sides with palms to floor.

Repeat 1, 2, 3 three times

4. Find a partner (see p. 34 for instructions on partner sequences). Stretch out arms, palms outward to partner, close to but not touching partner's palms. Consider this motion to be the forming of a flying heart, with one's heart at the centre and the arms as its wings. At a relaxed pace partners make a single circle clockwise round each other and come back to their original place, then progress to next partner by simply walking a few steps in their direction. This happens four times; with fourth and last partner progress, greet next partner but start again at 1, the 'Love, Love, Love' part of dance. That person will be your first partner for the next 'Allah' chorus.

HEALING PRAYER

By C.A. Sokoloff, Words By Inayat Khan

© Copyright 1987

*Note to Musicians: To simplify guitar accompaniment use capo on the
2nd fret and play: Am for Bm; G for A; and E for F#.*

HEALING PRAYER SONG & DANCE

from the Prayer 'Nayaz'

Music by C.A. Sokoloff (Nirtan)   *Words by Hazrat Inayat Khan*

I t is most beneficial for everyone, especially those on the Sufi path, to memorize the very moving healing prayer 'Nayaz' given by Hazrat Inayat Khan. By putting it to music, one can more easily remember this helpful and inspiring prayer and make use of it in one's life. By putting movements to the prayer one manifests a physical healing reality and brings healing energy to one's being and to others. In the dance this healing energy is first directed toward a healing of the self, then offered to others, individuals in one's life in need of healing and then outwards to larger spheres such as family, community and planet. The dancer attunes to Divine healing energy manifesting and available to all through the elements of nature, the sun, the air, and the life-force itself. It is suggested that before starting the dance, participants hold their hands up, palms out for a few minutes, feeling that healing energy come into their hands, increasing magnetism. It is this energy which can then be directed toward the mental, physical and spiritual healing of bodies, hearts and souls. The last line of Hazrat Inayat Khan's Healing Prayer is repeated as an affirmative chorus for a walking meditation. The dance usually starts and ends with this chorus. The chorus is repeated three times before the singing of the prayer itself. On the first repetition the healing energy can be directed toward self, on the second repetition toward an individual, and the third repetition, outward to a group, community, the city, country or planet. I usually end the dance with several repetitions of the affirmative chorus with a suggestion spoken for each such as (starting on the small level working to the large): for ourselves and those we love, for our families, for our community, for the forests, for the Middle East, for wherever there is suffering, for all who are in pain, for the planet, the cosmos etc. Individuals may wish to come in to the centre of the circle to absorb the healing energy created by the dance, and to rest there for a period of time during the dance.

HEALING PRAYER

LYRICS:
Chorus:
1. Heal, heal, heal
2. our bodies, hearts and souls,
3. our bodies, hearts and souls.
Prayer:
4. Beloved Lord,
5. Almighty God,
6. Through the rays of the sun,
7. Through the waves of the air,
8. Through the all-pervading life in space;
9. Purify
10. and revivify us
11. and we pray...(to chorus)

MOVEMENTS:

1. Begin in circle facing line of direction (to right or left at leader's discretion), having spent time magnetizing the hands, bring those hands down with palms towards floor, raise and lower hands 3 times as one sings the words 'heal, heal, heal', walking with very deliberate steps. The music and movements suggest almost a First Nations feeling to the walk, and the use of a simple drum beat or heartbeat is appropriate.

2. still walking, individuals can touch a part of their body in need of healing when singing 'our bodies'; hands to heart when singing 'hearts'; and arms upwards and spin when singing 'souls'

3. the same movements as 2, but this time do not spin on 'souls'
(Repeat 1, 2, 3 three times with a concentration first on healing of the self, then of another person, then of a larger group.)

4. Joining hands facing in to circle take small steps backward, bowing to the 'Beloved Lord'

HEALING PRAYER

5. take steps in to circle raising arms in joyous praise, looking heavenward

6. let go of hands, but keep arms raised, hands touching at thumb and index fingers, forming a triangle, a Zoroastrian sun sign, stepping backwards, let arms spread out like sun-rays

7. walking in the line of direction with free-flowing arm movements representing waves of the air

8. continue walking with free movements but add a turn

9. join hands in circle and come together in to the circle with great energy, arms raised, looking up

10. with energy, spin out

11. stand still in circle, in prayer posture, palms together in front of chest

Repeat Chorus.

I COME FROM A PERFECT SOURCE

By C.A. Sokoloff, Words By Inayat Khan

I COME FROM A PERFECT SOURCE
A Healing Affirmation
Music by C.A. Sokoloff (Nirtan)   *Words by Hazrat Inayat Khan*

This healing affirmation is taken from Hazrat Pir-o-Murshid Inayat Khan's teachings on healing in the Sufi Message volume on the subject. It was kindly brought to my attention by Shaikha Hamida Verlinden of Holland, the secretary of the International Sufi Movement, who demonstrated a series of arm movements to accompany the affirmation. Hamida suggested I might set the affirmation to music and turn it into a dance if I wished. However, it was only when one of our local Sufi community was diagnosed with a life-threatening disease that the music and dance movements came into being. In Volume IV, Health (p. 48) Hazrat Pir-o-Murshid Inayat Khan writes:

It is not selfish to think about one's health. No doubt it is undesirable to be thinking about one's illness all the time, to worry about it or to be too anxious about it; but to care about one's health is the most religious thing there is because it is the health of body and mind that enables one to do service to God and to one's fellow humans, by which one accomplishes one's life's purpose. One should think: I come from a perfect source and I am bound for a perfect goal, the light of the perfect Being is kindled in my soul. I live, move and have my being in God; and nothing in the world, of the past or present, has power to touch me, for I rise above all. It is this thought which will make one rise above influences of inharmony and disorder and will bring a person to the enjoyment of the greatest bliss in life, which is health.

I COME FROM A PERFECT SOURCE

LYRICS:
1. I come from a perfect source,
2. I'm bound for a perfect goal,
3. The light of the perfect Being
4. is kindled in my soul.
5. I live, move and have my being in God,
6. and nothing in the world of past or present
7. has the power to touch me
8. for I rise above all,
9. for I rise above all.

MOVEMENTS:
1. Hold hands in circle, move four steps in to centre, raising arms, looking up

2. moving backwards four steps bring arms down but eyes look up as if at the stars or the 'perfect goal'

3. releasing hands raise arms upward at sides, palms up, until hands are above head

4. hands come together above head to form a candle flame shape on 'kindled', and then hands move together down to heart on 'soul'

5. walking to the right in the line of direction, free movement as one is inclined

6. a spin and then facing outward

7. standing in place, circle facing outward, arms come up in an interpretive motion of protecting or blocking the self from external conditions, which each dancer can create according to their own inspiration

8. still facing outward, hands at shoulder level, palms down, forcibly push hands down toward the earth slowly, creating a sensation of rising up

9. hands scoop up with energy as dancers turn into the circle and repeat the motion of lowering hands with palms down.

Ishq' Allah Mabud L'illah
God is Love, Lover and Beloved
Words & Music by C.A.Sokoloff (Nirtan)

The Sufi chant Ishq' Allah Mabud L'illah (pronounced *ishk a lah ma bood lee lah*) has always been one of my favourites. It is a practice that inevitably brings a feeling of comfort and well-being, despite any conditions. With its focus on the Divine as Love, Lover and Beloved, it is particularly effective when dealing with feelings of loneliness, unworthiness or loss. The attunement is simply on the heart, and the love which streams forth from it and the Divine Love which, when emptied of self, the heart also receives. A strict pronunciation of the spoken *wazifa* (the names of the attributes of the Divine nature as chanted by Sufis) differs slightly from that offered above, however this version is especially musical. This dance should be gentle and moderate, and of the *jemal* or receptive quality. This is a song of love and a dance of love which we offer to the Divine and to each other. By attuning to the heart, we feel the presence of Divine Love and sense in our circle and partners the Divine Lover, showering us with love, and the Divine Beloved, whom we constantly seek through our relationships. The changing directions and back and forth movement of the dance mimics the poetic 'playing of hide and seek' which characterizes the spiritual journey of longing and aspiration.

ISHQ' ALLAH MABUD L'ILLAH

LYRICS:
1. Ishq' Allah
2. Mabud L'illah,
3. Ishq' Allah
4. Mabud L'illah,
5. Ishq' Allah Mabud L'illah,
6. L'illah, L'illah,
7. Ishq' Allah Mabud Lillah, Lillah.
8. God is Love
9. and the One who loves,
10. Love, Lover and Beloved.
11. Ishq' Allah Mabud Lillah,
12. L'illah, L'illah,
13. Ishq' Allah
14. Mabud L'illah, L'illah.

MOVEMENTS:
1. Stand in circle, hands joined at shoulder level (elbows bent). Lean right on 'ishq,' lean left on 'Allah'

2. take three small steps to the right using right foot, left foot, right foot

3. repeat 1 but start by leaning left first, then right

4. repeat 2 but moving to the left, using left foot, right foot, left foot on steps

5. repeat 1 and 2

6. move into the circle slowly with hands joined, raising arms in praise

7. releasing hands, spin toward left (counter-clockwise) back to place on circle, ending with hands on heart

ISHQ' ALLAH MABUD L'ILLAH

8. turning to partner (the direction in which one turns will also be the direction in which one progresses) extend right palm and touch palms (left hand remains on heart), looking deeply through the eyes into the soul, step toward partner with right foot on 'God is' and bring left foot together on 'Love'

9. stepping back from partner with left foot on 'and the one,' bringing right foot together on 'who loves,' right palm remains touching partner's

10. raising left arm, palm up, circle slowly with or around partner, still gazing in eyes, taking four steps starting with right foot (right, left, right, left) until partners have changed places with each other

11. repeat 8 and 9

12. repeat 10 but this time complete a single revolution and return back to original place

13. bow to partner with hands over heart, receiving the Divine love they have offered

14. progress to new partner by simply walking three steps, bringing hands from heart to palms upturned in front, offering Divine Love, greet briefly with the eyes, and turn into the circle.

ISHQ' ALLAH MABUD L'ILLAH

By C.A. Sokoloff

Open Our Hearts
from Prayer 'Khatum'

Music by C.A.Sokoloff (Nirtan)   *Words by Hazrat Inayat Khan*

This song and dance came into being out of discussion during a Sufi study circle meeting about how the reading of Inayat Khan's *Gathas* (instructional materials) was far more profound when we had fully prepared ourselves to receive these spiritual teachings. After leaving that meeting, I imagined that perhaps a song could be created which would be sung before these readings in order to open our minds and hearts to their deepest meanings. Simultaneously the lovely words from the Prayer Khatum and a simple melody came to mind, to fulfill this purpose. Soon after, it became clear that this music could also be used for a partner dance. When we tried out the dance at our next meeting, a deep and joyous ceremony of the open heart evolved, inspiring us in new directions.

The song consists of two verses (each of which are repeated) and a chorus (also repeated). In the dance, the voice from within is gleaned through the changing faces of 'the Beloved' as one greets and re-greets partners. The dance is somewhat unusual in that partners at first progress backwards (to their corner, the person at their back) and then progress forwards on the 'Ya Fatah' chorus. This may appear complex, but is actually simple to both explain and perform and results in a re-greeting of past partners, with the addition of new partners. The effect of this process is deeply engaging but can also be somewhat intoxicating. Dancer leaders may suggest that participants maintain their focus on the opening of the heart during the very joyous 'Ya Fatah' chorus.

OPEN OUR HEARTS

By C.A.Sokoloff, Words by Inayat Khan

© Copyright 1999

LYRICS:
1. Open our hearts
2. that we may hear Thy voice, which constantly
3. cometh from within. (Repeat 1, 2, 3)
4. Disclose to us Thy Divine Light
5. which is hidden
6. in our souls. (Repeat 4, 5, 6)
7. Ya Fatah, Ya Fatah, Ya, Fatah, Ya Fatah. (Repeat)

Open Our Hearts

MOVEMENTS:
Begin by standing in circle facing a partner, both hands on heart.
1. Turn to your corner (the person at your back), opening right hand out from heart, as you turn

2. Take hands with this new partner and looking in each other's eyes, slowly exchange places, travelling clockwise

3. Let go of hands and bow to each other with hands on heart.
Repeat 1, 2, 3 (with new corner) for the repetition of the 'Open our hearts...' verse

4. Turn to the next corner with right arm opening from heart, then raise both arms above head, palms out, and lower hands, massaging aura of partner, from crown to shoulders

5. Repeat movement 2, exchanging places

6. Repeat movement 3, bowing
Repeat 4, 5, 6 (with new corner) for the repetition of the 'Disclose to us...' verse

7. For this section instead of turning to 'corner' dancers proceed in the direction they are facing, first greeting person to whom they have just bowed, with hands to heart and stretching outwards. They then simply walk forward and greet next partner in the same way. Dancers progress and greet a partner on each 'Ya Fatah' (except the last), with opening movement of hands from heart. On the eighth and last 'Ya Fatah' they do not progress but spin in place. (If dancers are experienced, a spin can also be incorporated on the fourth 'Ya Fatah', either while progressing or in place). Return to 'Open our hearts...'

To end the dance allow the 'Ya Fatah' chorus to continue so dancers greet everyone around the circle. Then sing only the line 'Open our hearts, that we may hear thy voice...' prolonging that note, everyone facing the centre of the circle, extending hands from heart.

ALLAH HU
Zikar Dance for Whirling
Music by C.A. Sokoloff (Nirtan)

The traditional dance of the Sufis is the ancient dervish whirling, also known as turning or spinning. This practice is said to originate in the movements of the 13th century mystic poet Mevlana Jelaluddin Rumi of Persia who, lost in the thought of his master Shams e Tabriz, revolved around a pole in his academy, speaking of his longing in verse. Despite being somewhat unusual under normal circumstances, such turning seems nevertheless to be a very natural motion for human beings. As children, many of us enjoyed such whirling, something that confirmed my own attraction for the Sufi path. While the Mevlevi Order, founded by the Sufi poet, has passed along a beautiful, complex turning ceremony known as the Sema, requiring great discipline and practice, the simple action of spinning in place, following a few basic guidelines, can be done by almost anyone and offers great benefits. Whirling leads to ecstasy as one begins to feel that one is, in fact, standing still while the world revolves around one (as indeed it does). One feels a part of the cycle of creation and can be literally lifted into the highest spheres. Afterwards one feels deeply attuned, contented, and inspired. One notices a new clarity of vision and may also find that mystic poetry comes through one effortlessly. Whirling can be done for long periods of time without experiencing dizziness, however this dance offers a mere introduction to the practice. The chant 'Allah Hu' (pronounced Al-lah-hoo, roughly translated as 'the One Who Is') invokes the one and only Divine Being. These ancient syllables resound in the heart and are potent sounds whose vibratory quality transcends language and traditions. The Sufis have a saying: Say Allah and Allah you become! The song utilizes three melodic cycles, each repeated four times.

ALLAH HU

C minor drone

By C.A. Sokoloff

Al- lah Hu   Al- lah Hu   Al- lah

Hu   Al- lah Hu   Al- lah Hu Al- lah Hu

Hu   Hu   Hu   Hu

Instructions for informal Sufi Whirling:

The centre of concentration is the heart. The sound 'hu' (hooo), the Sufi's hidden name of God, can be blown into the heart and sustained as long as turning continues.

Cross arms and place hands on shoulders, the right over the left or place hands on heart, in similar fashion. Begin to slowly pivot to the left (counter-clockwise), left toe keeping in place, right foot pivoting around it as one begins to turn, slowly. Keep eyes open, but do not focus on anything, keep glance steady and simply watch the world go by.

Allow the hands to gradually come away from the shoulders or heart as turning continues. The right palm is held up, receiving Divine Energy, which then travels through the heart and through the left arm. The left palm is held down, releasing Divine Energy to earth.

Keep to a pace which is natural and comfortable for you. If you feel inclined to speed up, do so, but continue to centre in the heart, maintaining the sound 'hu' and with steady glance taking in the circling world. Allow arms to move of themselves. Moving the head even slightly can bring about a sensation of ecstasy. Should dizziness occur, simply slow down the turn.

Finish turning by gradually slowing down until such time as the world stops revolving. At that time, stop in one place, cross arms over chest, hands on shoulders, and bow head. Now close eyes and gaze inward. Take some minutes to assimilate the experience.

ALLAH HU

LYRICS:
1. Allah hu, Allah hu, Allah hu, Allah hu,
2. Allah hu, Allah hu, Allah hu, Allah hu,
3. Allah hu, Allah hu, Allah hu, Allah hu.

4. Hu..... Hu.....Hu..... Hu......

MOVEMENTS;
1. Stand in circle, hands joined at shoulder level, elbows bent. Take step to right on 'Al-' , bring left foot together on 'lah', do same to left on 'hu' (step left and close with right). Head leans or rolls in direction of movement in zikar fashion (from left to right shoulder across chest continuing from right to left in back).

2. Circle turns to face right and travels in line of direction, right arm on left shoulder of person in front, left hand on heart, step right and close, leaning outward, on 'Allah', and step left and close, leaning inward on 'hu', blowing 'hu' into centre of circle.

3. Facing into circle, hands joined, elbows back, right foot steps in to circle and left foot comes together, arms moving up, head up on 'Allah', and reverse (left steps back, right together, arms down, head down on 'Hu').

Leader may select or dancers may volunteer to try whirling in centre of circle for a portion of the dance (see Whirling Instructions). When a person has completed whirling and taken some moments to regain composure, they may wish to form a pole just inside the circle and keep up the rhythmic 'Hu' (4), repeated every four beats, standing still, hands on heart, blown into heart. There can be some movement between these positions as the dance continues, although it should be done as unobtrusively as possible so that the energy is sustained.

Bismillah, Ya Rahman Er Rahim

Music by Hidayat Inayat-Khan   *Dance by Nirtan*

This dance uses some of the beautiful music for *wazifa* practice created by Pir Hidayat Inayat-Khan who, in addition to his role as leader of the International Sufi Movement, is an extraordinary composer of modern symphonic music. The music demands a strict adherence to rhythm and a pause of two beats between the sacred words. A recorded version is available on a set of CD's of Pir Hidayat's music for *wazifa* practice recently released by Shaikh Jelaluddin Gary Sill of Banff, Alberta (c/o Sound of Light, Box 490 Banff, Alberta, Canada, ToL oCo). The movements of this dance are taken from a middle-eastern blessing gesture. The phrase 'Bismillah, Ya Rahman, Er Rahim' (pronounced bis-mill-ah, ya rahk-mon, air-rakh-heem) is the opening of Islam's Holy Scripture, Koran, normally translated, "In the name of Allah, who is Mercy and Compassion." Through the repetition of this *wazifa*, the qualities of Divine Mercy and Divine Compassion are affirmed, leading to a condition of peace and serenity. The dance embodies the receiving of these Divine qualities from on high, holding them in the heart and then humbly offering them to the world.

BISMILLAH, YA RAHMAN, ER RAHIM

C drone   By Hidayat Inayat Khan

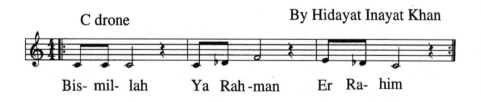

Bis- mil- lah   Ya Rah -man   Er Ra- him

© Copyright 1999, Hidayat Inayat-Khan

Bismillah Ya Rahman, Er Rahim

LYRICS:
1. Bismillah,
2. Ya Rahman,
3. Er Rahim

MOVEMENTS:

1. Begin with two circles, preferably of equal numbers, one inside the other; the inside circle facing the outside circle. Each person faces a partner. On 'Bismillah' everyone raises their arms and reaches to sky, looking up, acknowledging the Divine Presence.

2. on 'Ya Rahman' each person brings both hands to their heart, looking in their partners eyes, reflecting Divine Mercy.

3. On 'Erahim' the hands simply open, coming down to sides, the palms out, experiencing Divine Compassion. The head bows. In the 2-beat pause, each circle takes a single step to the right, ready to begin again with a new partner.

To end: Both circles can turn outwards for several repetitions, blessing the outer community and end by both circles turning inwards and slowing down after two repetitions and stopping in the final blessing posture.

BISMILLAH GREETING
Music and Dance by C.A. Sokoloff (Nirtan)

This dance has been created for the 23rd annual Northwest Sufi camp (in Washington state) or as a greeting or welcoming dance for any large gathering. It uses the Koran's opening word 'Bismillah' ('We begin in the name of Allah'), which is sung to a simple, joyous melody. The dance is done in two circles, facing each other, moving in opposite directions. It can start with four or more simple repetitions of the sacred *zikar* phrase 'Allah Hu' (God alone exists), to establish the walking rhythm, after which the 'Bismillah' chorus is performed. After each chorus there is a verse invoking the Divine qualities of Mercy & Compassion ('Ya Rahman, Er Rahim') and Divine Peace ('Ya Salaam Aleykum'; translated 'May peace be with you' and pronounced 'ya-sal-aam-al-leh-koom'). The movements of the dance are simple and there are several variations possible, as suggested in the instructions. If there are not enough dancers for two circles, the dance can be done with one circle using a choreographed partner progression of the leader's choice or a free greeting of partners on the 'Ya Rahman' verse.

BISMILLAH
By C.A. Sokoloff

Bis- mil- lah   Bis- mil- lah   Bis- mil

-lah   Bis- mil- lah   Bis -mil

Bismillah Greeting Dance

LYRICS:
Spoken: Allah hu, Allah hu, Allah hu, Allah hu.

Chorus:
1. Bismillah, Bismillah, Bismillah, Bismillah,
   Bismillah, Bismillah, Bismillah, Bismillah,
2. Bismillah, Bismillah, Bismillah, Bismillah, Bismillah, Bismillah
3. Bismillah, Bismillah.

4. Ya Rahman, Er Rahim, Bismillah, Bismillah,
   Ya Rahman, Er Rahim, Bismillah, Bismillah.
5. Ya Salaam Aleykum, Bismillah, Bismillah,
   Ya Salaam Aleykum,
6. Bismillah, Bismillah.
Chorus

MOVEMENTS:
Begin holding hands in two circles which face each other. Circles can walk to right while saying 'Allah Hu' to establish pace.
1. Each circle walks to their right at a moderate pace, starting on right foot, greeting with glance dancers in the other circle.

2. Changing directions, each circle now moves to their left.

3. Spin to left (counter-clockwise) in place

4. Take hands of someone facing you in the other circle and begin to move around each other in a counter-clockwise circle

5. Still holding hands with partner, change direction and move in a clockwise circle.

6. Return to original place and spin.
Again form two circles for the 'Bismillah' chorus.

BISMILLAH GREETING DANCE

End by repeating Chorus more than once.

Note: The greeting part of this dance is quite informal. If numbers are uneven, the small circles on the 'Ya Rahman' verse can consist of any number of dancers. In addition, leaders can encourage dancers to try to find new people to greet during these verses.

Variations:
The pace of the steps need not stay sedate. The leader can instruct dancers to walk in double-time. The tempo of the music remains unchanged, but the number of steps taken by dancers is doubled.

On the 'Ya Rahman' verse, some partners may choose to spin together quickly, crossing hands for stability and speed.

The leader may choose to insert repetitions of the 'Allah Hu' chant, either walking in direction, or side-stepping to the right, with zikar-like head motion up and down into heart. Or the leader may wish to create a third inner circle to maintain this chant throughout the entire dance.

I touch Thy life in movement
and feel Thy spirit in stillness.

Every movement of nature
is a signal from Thee.

Let me see Thy Divine movement
in all moving things of the Universe.

Let me see the secret
hidden behind Thy movement.

Hazrat Inayat Khan,
from Nature Meditations

Part Two

Songs and Dances
from the Nature Meditations

'The Nature Meditations' of Hazrat Pir-o-Murshid Inayat Khan is an exquisite collection of aphorisms, offered by the Master for contemplation of the Divine Presence in nature. This volume (Omega Publications) has long been a favourite of mine and I have worn out several versions through constant use. Each meditation is offered as a sentence in two parts, one part for contemplation during the inhalation of a breath, and the other for the exhalation. When set to music this form naturally results in the age-old tradition of call and response, or question and answer, found particularly in Eastern musical styles. Students of Hazrat Inayat Khan and his descendants have frequently set to music the lovely aphorisms contained in his masterpiece *Gayan, Vadan, Nirtan*; however, *The Nature Meditations*, while equally appropriate for this purpose, have remained, so to speak, hidden between the covers of the book. These became a most inspiring source for new Sufi songs and dances. Very often a few related aphorisms on a particular subject have been put together to create the verse of a song. Once again, inspiration directed the selection and placement of the texts and revealed their melodies.

"Worship God in Nature," Hazrat Pir-o-Murshid Inayat Khan writes in *Gayan, Vadan, Nirtan* and includes as one of the Ten Sufi Thoughts, "There is one holy book, the sacred manuscript of nature, the only scripture which can enlighten the reader." *The Nature Meditations* were dictated by Pir-o-Murshid to his secretary during the very first Sufi Summer School in Wissous, France, 1921. They offer a peaceful experience of the mystic's oneness with nature, during which the presence of the Divine Beloved is perceived in all. "Every soul born with a mystical tendency is constantly drawn towards nature," writes Inayat, "for in nature that soul finds its life's demand."

AWAKE, MY SOUL, TO THE CALL

Music by C.A.Sokoloff (Nirtan)   *Words by Hazrat Inayat Khan*

This is a meditative, walking dance preparing the dancer to listen and receive 'the call of the Spirit of Guidance.' According to Murshid Shamcher Bryn Beorse, a student of Hazrat Pir-o-Murshid Inayat Khan, the concept of 'the Spirit of Guidance' is one of the great achievements of Inayat's Sufi Message. It is a concept the mystic was able to introduce and yet leave largely undefined, allowing the student to receive through attunement, meditation and inner development, a personal understanding of this ever-present guiding spirit. This dance invites participants to attune, reflect and open oneself to receive the call of the Spirit of Guidance for the fulfillment of one's life purpose. The Sufi concept of the 'awakening' of the soul from the slumber induced by the distracting world of sensation, invites the dancer to explore the inner self, creating the capacity for the Divine Presence within to manifest, "as the light filleth the crescent moon."

Awake! For morning in the Bowl of Night
Has flung the Stone that puts the
Stars to flight:
And Lo! The Hunter of the East has caught
The Sultan's Turret in a Noose of Light!
Rubaiyat, Omar Khayyam

AWAKE MY SOUL TO THE CALL

By C.A.Sokoloff,Words By Inayat Khan

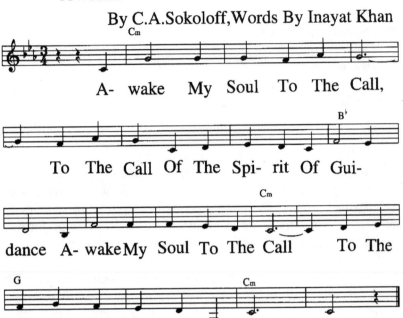

A- wake My Soul To The Call,

To The Call Of The Spi- rit Of Gui-

dance A- wake My Soul To The Call To The

Call Of The Spi- rit Of Gui- dance

© Copyright 1992

Note to Musicians:
To simplify the chords for guitar, place capo on the 3rd fret and play:
A minor for Cm, G for B Flat, and E for G.

AWAKE MY SOUL TO THE CALL

LYRICS:
1. Awake, my soul, to the call,
2. to the call of the Spirit
3. of Guidance.
1. Awake, my soul, to the call,
2. to the call of the Spirit
3. of Guidance.

MOVEMENTS:
The song and dance are in 3/4 or waltz time, and the movements follow this rhythm (ie. stepping in 3 beats, such as right, together, pause; left, together, pause). The dance is done in a cycle of three primary movements which are repeated consecutively. Each cycle is performed during an entire repetition of the verse, as suggested above.

Cycle One: Walking in line of direction. Hands are beside the ears with palms forward, in listening pose. Step with right foot, left together, pause; then left foot, right together, pause and continue in this fashion

3. Whenever the words 'of guidance' are sung, there is a single spin in place to the right, and continue actions for cycle until next 3.

Cycle Two: Joining hands in the circle sway, stepping right, together, pause; then left, together, pause; and continue adding the spin on 3.

Cycle Three: With hands joined circle rocks forward and back (step in with right, left together, pause; step back with left, right together, pause) and repeat until the spin on 3 and continue in wave motion. Repeat cycles one, two and three as appropriate.

Finish with cycle three, moving forward and back in the circle and repeat last line, 'to the Call of the Spirit of Guidance' a few times, slowing down for the final time and completing spin with hands on heart. Allow some minutes of silence for personal reflection on the meaning of the dance.

IT IS THOU WHOM I SEE

Music by C.A. Sokoloff (Nirtan)   *Words by Hazrat Inayat Khan*

To the eyes of the mystic, all aspects of life reveal the Divine Presence—audible in the sounds of life, visible in various guises and forms, to be worshipped in each individual with whom one comes in contact. Even one's own self is no longer one's own, when conscious of the Divine Source at the root of one's being. The Sufis say that God is closer than the jugular vein, or in Hazrat Inayat Khan's words used here, "Thou art closer to me than myself." In this dance some move around the circle changing places, while others remain in place. But everyone experiences the changing names and forms of the Divine Reality.

Every sound I hear is Thine own voice.
In the fragrance I smell the perfume of Thy spirit.
In every word spoken to me I hear Thy voice, my Lord.
All that touches me is Thine own touch.
In everything that I taste I experience the syrup
                              of Thy delicious spirit.
In every place I recognize Thee, my Lord.
Every word that touches my ears is Thy message.
Everything that touches me thrills me with the joy of Thy kiss.
Wherever I roam I meet Thee,
Wherever I reach I find Thee, my Lord.
Wherever I look I see Thy glorying face;
Whatever I touch, I touch Thy beloved hand.
Whomever I see, I see Thee in his soul.
From whomever I take anything, I take it from Thee.
Whomever I give something, I give it humbly to Thee.
Whoever cometh to me, to me it is Thy call.
To whomever I call, I call at Thine own gate.
Whenever I nod to anyone, I bow before Thy throne.
In showing my sympathy to anyone,
I express my love to Thee, my Beloved.
                    Hazrat Inayat Khan, Nature Meditations

IT IS THOU WHOM I SEE

By C.A. Sokoloff, Words By Inayat Khan

© Copyright 1994

Note to Musicians:
To simplify guitar accompaniment place capo on the 2nd fret and play:
Am for Bm; G for A; and F for G.

IT IS THOU WHOM I SEE

LYRICS:
1. It is Thou
2. whom I see
3. in all names and forms. (repeat 1, 2, 3 three times)
4. Thou art closer to me than myself. (repeat verse)
5. Let my spirit reflect, my Beloved, the beauty of Thy
6. colour and form (repeat 5 & 6)

MOVEMENTS:
1. To begin: Start by holding hands in circle. The dance leader can count off round the circle, naming the first person 'Allah' and the next person, 'Hu' and continuing all around the circle. The 'Allahs' will move in the first part of the dance, while the 'Hu's' remain in place. On 'It is Thou', the Allah's release their left hand and walk and stand in front of the person on their right, taking both their hands.

2. On the word 'see', partners bow slightly to each other, acknowledging and affirming the Divine Presence reflected in each other's being

3. 'Allah's' release the right hand and proceed to other side of partner, circle comes together again holding hands.

4. Take four small steps (one on each beat) into circle, raising arms and hands, and four steps out again, lowering arms and hands

Repeat section (1, 2, 3; 1, 2, 3; 1, 2, 3, 4)

5. Let go of hands, circle walks to right, holding arms up, slightly to the left, palms in to circle as if reflecting Divine Light

6. Spin to left.

Repeat section 5 changing direction; then 6 and return to 1.

I SEE THY BELOVED BEAUTY

Music by C.A.Sokoloff (Nirtan)   *Words by Hazrat Inayat Khan*

A joyous dance in which we circle with partners experiencing the dizzying array of colours in life. The second part of the dance simply uses the sound 'Hu', the hidden name of God which all of nature constantly repeats, from the trees blowing in the wind, to the music of the spheres circling in the cosmos. Be sure to keep centred in the heart, attuned to the Divine Presence which sometimes thrills one with an experience of ecstasy.

I SEE THY BELOVED BEAUTY
By C.A. Sokoloff, Words By Inayat Khan

I See Thy Be- lov- ed Beau- ty

In All Col- ours And Forms I See Thy Be-

lov- ed Beau-ty In All Col- ours And Forms

Hu- Hu---

I SEE THY BELOVED BEAUTY

LYRICS:
1. I see Thy beloved beauty
2. in all colours and forms.
3. I see Thy beloved beauty
4. in all colours and forms. (Repeat 1, 2, 3, 4)
5. Hu............ 6. Hu.............
7. Hu............
8. Hu............

MOVEMENTS:
1. Start in circle, facing a partner. Dancers will progress in the direction in which they are initially facing. Partners circle around each other clockwise (taking four steps), holding hands and looking in each other's eyes.

2. Partners let go of hands and each spins counter-clockwise (to left).

3. Partners take hands again and circle around each other in reverse direction (counter-clockwise), taking four steps.

4. Partners release hands and each spins once to the left, and then progresses by walking in direction to next partner.

5. Everyone in circle (or two circles for large groups) with hands on shoulders of person on either side of them. Circle walks right.

6. Continue walking right.

7. Continue walking but reverse directions (walking left)

8. Everyone spins.

LET ME BECOME THY BODY

Music by C.A.Sokoloff (Nirtan)   *Words by Hazrat Inayat Khan*

In the *Nature Meditations* concerning the Sage or Holy Being, this affirmation is found. Through it we identify with the Holy One, who identifies with the Divine, that our body may become the receptacle for the sage's Divine Wisdom and our soul, the soul of the Sage. As in so many of Inayat's touching aphorisms the 'Thy' and the 'my' are constantly in play, allowing one the opportunity to exchange for the personal ego, the Divine essence. For the purpose of the dance I have added as a chorus the Hebrew exaltation, *kadosh,* (pronounced ka-doash) meaning 'holy'; as holiness is the subject of this meditation. In the Jewish tradition the angels of heaven are constantly engaged in the repetition of this word. "Kadosh, kadosh, kadosh," they chant; "Holy, Holy, Holy is the Lord of Hosts. The whole world is filled with His glory." It is interesting to muse on the meaning of this word. In our English language it can be seen as relating to our word for 'wholeness,' indicating Divine Perfection. In Hebrew it also invokes the ancient Egyptian word for soul or spirit, the 'ka.' The *kadosh* section of the dance is one of free movement and celebration, where dancers float like angels on high engaged in the praise of the Holy One.

Let me Become Thy Body

LYRICS:
1. Let me become Thy body, Thou become my spirit,
2. O Holy One, O Holy One, O Holy One
3. O Holy One. (Repeat 1, 2, 3)
4. Kadosh, kadosh, kadosh, kadosh, kadosh, kadosh. (Repeat)

MOVEMENTS:
Start by holding hands in circle. Leader can count off around circle (Allah, Hu, Allah, Hu, etc.) Allah's will travel on movement 2 while Hu's remain in place.
1. Circle begins by doing modified grapevine step to right (step to side with right foot, left foot crosses in front, step to side with right foot, left foot crosses behind)

2. Allah's release the left hand and move in front of person on their right, taking both their hands. Both offer a slight greeting nod, acknowledging the Divine Presence of 'the Holy One' in the person before them. Then Allah's release the right hand and travel to the right of that person, joining the circle again. This movement is completed during the singing of the phrase 'Oh holy One' and repeated two more times as that phrase is sung. (Three people have been thus greeted.)

3. On the fourth repetition of 'Oh Holy One' everyone spins in place.

4. On the 'Kadosh' chorus, dancers move freely around the room embodying the angelic hosts of heaven. This can be joyous, exuberant movement, arms reaching up and out from heart, or any other gesture a dancer may choose. By the end of the second repetition of the chorus it is necessary to return to the circle, in such a way that Allah's and Hu's are alternating as before. For this purpose, suggest that when the Hu's return to the circle they do so with arms held high above head in praise, and Allah's place themselves between two Hu's. Ask that dancers remain centred and divinely guided to smoothly accomplish this transition. End the dance with an extended 'kadosh' chorus of free movement.

LET ME BECOME

By C.A. Sokoloff, Words By Inayat Khan

LET EVERY MOVEMENT OF LIFE

Music by C.A. Sokoloff (Nirtan)   *Words by Hazrat Inayat Khan*

This dance combines several of the beautiful *Nature Meditations,* with a focus on all movement as the dance of Divine Love. In nature the mystic attunes to the Divine Beloved, who is hidden in all things. Once again the exchange of the 'Thy' and the 'My' becomes a practice of surrendering the limited self in the Divine Spirit. This dance is a waltz (3/4 time) from start to finish, and the movements as choreographed are very lovely, but may take some practise. Some groups may prefer simply to use it as a free-form waltz for partners — waltzing being 'whirling for two.' Either way, a waltz-type step, or three-step is needed. The feet move right, together, right; left, together, left — or right, left, right; left, right, left.

LYRICS:
1. Let every movement of life
2. whisper Thy name to my ears.
3. Unveil Thy face, Beloved,
4. that I may behold Thy vision.
5. Let my self turn into Thy Being,
6. Let my life become Thy Soul.
7. Let me lose myself
8. In Thy consciousness.
9. Oh let me lose myself
10. in Thy consciousness.

MOVEMENTS:
To begin: Form a circle and find partners. Have dancers note the direction in which they turn to find partner. It is also the direction in which they will walk for the partner progression.
1. Holding hands in circle, 3-step in to circle and out, with arms moving up and down in wave-like motion, while moving circle to the right. Starting with right foot move: In-2-3, out-2-3, in-2-3, out-2-3

LET EVERY MOVEMENT IN LIFE

2. Release hands and still using 3-step do a single spin to the right, with hands palm forward at the level of the ears, in listening pose.

3. Still using 3-step, move in towards centre of the circle, hands rising in front of face, and lifting up above head, as if lifting a veil.

4. A single spin to left (3-step), moving back out to circle, hands lowering as if pulling down a curtain to reveal the Beloved

5. Turning to partner extend right palm, elbow bent. Touch palms and circle halfway around each other clockwise, using 3-step

6. Changing hands, touching left palms, reverse direction and come back to starting place

7. Progress by walking to next partner and repeat 5

8. Repeat 6

9. Progress to next partner and greet briefly but return to circle. Holding hands, circle 3-steps to right, then left, right again, left again

10. Two spins to right. And repeat from 1.

LET EVERY MOVEMENT OF LIFE

By C.A. Sokoloff, Words By Inayat Khan

Part Three

Related Heart Songs & Dances

In this section are some songs and dances which stem from various inclinations of the heart, related to the Sufi way or for specific celebrations. Some may borrow a line from the teachings of Hazrat Inayat Khan, others are simply in the spirit of the Sufi Message. Some use the Arabic language *wazifas*, or names of the qualities of God, as practiced by Sufis. Others are entirely in English; but all share in the heart quality which the Sufi strives to develop. Many of the songs continue in the atmosphere of the *Nature Meditations*.

PEACE IS THE LONGING OF EVERY SOUL

Music & words by C.A. Sokoloff (Nirtan)

This song and dance emerged from an invitation to lead a dance at a re-dedication of a 'Peace Pole.' These are markers which are 'planted' at locations around the globe as an affirmation of peace throughout the planet. The song borrows a quotation from Hazrat Inayat Khan that, "Peace is the longing of every soul." It also invokes sacred phrases and practices from several world religions and cultures: the Hebrew greeting *Shalom* (pronounced sha-loam), meaning peace; from the Arabic, the *wazifa*, *Ya Salaam* (pronounced ya sallawm), meaning 'O Divine Peace;' the joyous Sanskrit affirmation of peace, *Om Shanti Om* (pronounced oam shawn-tee-oam); and the Buddhist practice of the 'long breath of peace.' Since so much of the unrest in today's world is the result of lack of understanding, tolerance and cooperation between followers of various traditions, it is hoped by including elements of many paths in a single song and dance, and by relating this hope for peace from the personal to the planetary level, this deep desire for peace may be realized on earth. This truly is a Dance of Universal Peace. The singing should be peaceful, and the movements as well—all elements very gentle and relaxed, without any strain if possible.

The idea for a dance using the sacred words for Divine Peace in both Hebrew and Arabic first emerged in autumn 1977 when the historic Peace Agreement between Israel and Egypt was signed. At that time I was staying in Banefsha's 'Three Rings' house in San Francisco, dedicated to peace in the Middle East. This mission had been begun by Murshid Samuel Lewis, the creator of the Dances of Universal Peace, and as I thought about such a dance, I felt his inspiration assisting its development. As is sometimes the case, however, it took nearly twenty years for this dance to actually manifest (indeed, the making of peace also takes patience and effort). Working in my living room on a recent summer afternoon, putting the finishing touches on this dance, I was startled by a bird that flew through my open front door. Disturbed at first, I later felt it had something to do with the spirit of Murshid Sam, welcoming this dance at last.

PEACE IS THE LONGING OF EVERY SOUL

By C.A. Sokoloff

Peace is the Longing of Every Soul

LYRICS:
1. Peace is the longing of every soul,
2. Shalom, Shalom, Shalom.
3. Peace is the longing of every soul,
4. Divine Peace, Ya Salaam.
5. Peace on the planet,
6. Peace in our homes,
7. Peace in our hearts,
8. Om Shanti Om!
9. Peace is the longing of every soul,
10. Shalom, Ya Salaam.
11. (spoken) With a long breath of peace. (repeat 4 times)

MOVEMENTS:
Before You Begin: Find a partner (a person on the left or right) and also note your 'corner' (the person on your other side). The direction in which one moves to greet partner is the direction in dancers progresses during the brief partner sequence of this dance.

1. Standing in circle, hands joined and held (elbows bent) at shoulder level; sway to the right (on 'Peace') and left (on 'longing'), right (on 'every') and left (on 'soul')

2. Turn upper body to partner and extend hands from heart, palms up, on first 'Shalom', greeting with eyes and offering peace; on second 'shalom' repeat gesture towards circle, and on third 'shalom' turn upper body and repeat gesture to 'corner.'

3. Back in circle, repeat 1

4. On 'Divine Peace' spin and progress to place beside next partner, on 'Ya Salaam' face circle and perform bowing gesture, left hand on heart, right hand touches head and rises, palm upward as head nods forward.

PEACE IS THE LONGING OF EVERY SOUL

5. Starting with right foot, taking small slow steps in to circle, hands down at sides, slightly in front, palms down

6. Continue steps in to circle and raise arms until fingertips meet over head, forming a roof of a 'home'

7. Stepping slowly backwards, bring joined palms to centre of forehead (third eye) on 'peace', and then to heart (palms still joined) on 'heart'

8. Continuing backwards with hands still at heart, bring forehead forward to rest on fingertips, connecting heart and third eye.

9. repeat 1

10. spin once in place on 'shalom' and repeat bowing gesture described in 4 on 'Ya Salaam'

11. Standing still with hands in front of body at level of navel, hands cradled in each other palms up, right hand over left, breathe consciously during the four repetitions of 'With a long breath of peace.' This phrase may be spoken by leader or other appointed person, or spoken only a few times and simply 'breathed' henceforth. Or the speaking of each repetition of the phrase may travel around the circle in a chosen direction, so that peace is affirmed with many different voices. The phrase may also be sung to either a melody improvised by one or many voices, or to the melody recorded on the CD accompanying this book. During this part of the dance musicians should continue the chord pattern indicated in the music.

To End: Repeat 10 a few times and 11 as well, if desired, breath and voice becoming progressively more refined and quiet until only 'peace' remains.

SONG OF TREES
Music & words by C.A. Sokoloff (Nirtan)   Dance by Sufia (Carol Sill)

This is a song about the need to combat the dire problem of the desertification of the planet through the planting of trees. In 1980 I was privileged to meet Richard 'St. Barbe' Baker, known as the 'Man of Trees' for his tireless work planting millions of trees throughout the planet, in order to prevent erosion of arable land. Hearing I was a songwriter, St. Barbe asked me to write a song for tree-planting, suggesting it would be a kind of march. That is not exactly how the song came to me, however.

On my journey to the very first Lake O'Hara Rocky Mountain Sufi camp (in 1980), I found myself delayed at the Calgary train station, waiting for the train that would carry my into the mountains. I waited outside near the platform on a lovely sunny day, carrying a small bamboo flute a friend had made. Blowing into the flute a melody came forth, and soon afterwards the words to go with it. When I finally arrived at the magnificent Lake O'Hara it was evening, and after settling in my cabin I had a most unusual experience. From outside I heard a low chorus humming the very song I had apparently 'written' that afternoon. In my bathrobe I went out to the water's edge to see if I could find the source of the etheric chorus, wondering how it was anyone could be singing that music when I had not yet shared it with a soul. In the stillness of the dreaming lake, surrounded by magnificent mountains, I realized that indeed it was the trees and elementals who had shared that music with me. Years later, Shaikha Sufia Carol Sill was asked to lead a dance at a Sufi gathering and she was inspired to create these movements to accompany the song. Since then the song and dance have travelled far and wide I am told, and people believe the song to be a folk-song that has long been around. Perhaps it is, but a tree-folk song.

This is a relatively simple dance, suitable for novices. Attune to the Divine Blessing we receive through the trees, who add beauty to our landscape, purify our air, prevent our soil from blowing away and humbly offer themselves for our needs. Consider the tree as a symbol of all elements in nature—feet rooted in the earth, sap coursing through its veins, the sun's fire stored within and accessed for heat and light, branches and leaves blowing in the air, reaching up to heaven. When there is a genuine appreciation of the helpful role played by trees in our life on earth, humanity will cease it's squandering of this precious resource.

LYRICS:
1. We plant a seed
2. and we grow a tree,
3. How beautiful, how beautiful, how beautiful, how beautiful.
4. And deserts dry,
5. Will bloom again
6. In greenery,
7. How beautiful, how beautiful, how beautiful,
8. the trees.

MOVEMENTS:
1. Begin in circle, holding hands. Circle steps backwards into a bow

2. circle steps in, arms raised

3. Let go hands and side-step to right, arms circling, left to right and around, like trees blowing in wind. On each 'how beautiful' take one side-step and do one arm circle. Add an extra step and circle after the last 'how beautiful'

4. Holding hands, the circle moves back, emptying of self in bow

5. Spirited movement in to centre of circle, arms raised

6. Joyous spin outward

7. repeat side-step and arm circles as described in 3, but for only three repetitions

8. release hands, standing still, bring palms together at heart, feeling rooted like a tree.

SONG OF TREES

Words and Music by C.A. Sokoloff

We Plant A Seed And We Grow A Tree How

Beau -ti -ful How Beau- ti- ful How Beau- ti- ful How

Beau- ti- ful And Des- erts Dry Will Bloom A- gain In

Green- e- ry How Beau- ti- ful How Beau- ti- ful How

Beau- ti- ful The Trees

© Copyright 1980

AT ONE WITH THE ESSENCE OF ALL

Music & words by C.A. Sokoloff (Nirtan)

This song and dance is a meditation on the five elements in the Sufi metaphysical understanding of nature and creation. These elements are: Earth, Water, Fire, Air and Ether. Ether is conceived to be the source and goal of all other elements. In the Sufi Element celebration (or *Ziraat* ceremony), it is described as "Ether, Essence of All." Ether can thus represent that living spirit that infuses all of nature. The song emerges from walking along the mountain trails of the inspiring Lake O'Hara region of the Canadian Rockies where the Canadian Sufi camp has been held for the past twenty years. When dancing visualize the healing influence of the elements described and place yourself mentally in the brilliant landscape of high mountains and clear skies, feeling the heat of a warming sun on one's skin, hearing the sound of a refreshing waterfall, and breathing in the intoxicating fragrance of pine trees in the Alpine Meadow.

This is good dance to invite free movement, while making use of a few element gestures used in some Zoroastrian-inspired dances— for Earth, hands at side with palms parallel to earth; for Water, hands above left shoulder cascading in waterfall motion to hip level on right; for Fire, ascending motion of right and left hands, clapping as right hand rises above head; for Air, arms fully extended to sides, slightly raised, but palms down; for Ether, a spin. Some ways of using these gestures are suggested in the movement instructions. Once again, the dance is in waltz time and a 3-step works best.

AT ONE

LYRICS:
1. With my feet, I walk upon the Earth,
2. Water falls beside me and the Air
3. is fragrant in the fire of the sunlight,
4. I'm at one with the Essence   5. of All.
6. Warm gold stones,
7. the water clear and cold.
8. Hot sun rays through sky   9. all bright and blue,
10. breathing in the Spirit of Nature
11. I'm at one with the Essence of All,
12. at one with the Essence of All.

MOVEMENTS:
1. Begin in circle facing line of direction hands beside hips, palms down (Earth gesture). Begin moving in 3-step, swinging hands from one side to the other along with leading foot (four swings)

2. Continue 3-step in direction bringing arms from high above left shoulder, cascading down towards right hip (Water gesture), then again from right to left (repeat sequence)

3. Take a turn to right, right arm rising above head and left hand clapping along the way (Fire gesture)

4. Holding hands move towards centre of circle, arms lifted

5. Spin out to left, moving back to circle

6. Repeat 1 (minus repetitions)   7. Repeat 2 (minus repetitions)
8. Repeat 3
9. Continue 3-step in direction with arms extended, palm up (Air)

10. holding hands facing centre of circle, sway right and left (repeat)

11. & 12. repeat 4 and 5.

AT ONE

By C.A. Sokoloff

With My Feet I Walk Up- on The Earth

Wa- ter -falls Be- side Me And The Air Is

Fra- grant In The Fi- re Of The Sun- light I'm At

One With The Es- sence Of All All At

One With The Es- sence Of All.

Oh the Beauty, Oh the Wonder

Music & words by C.A. Sokoloff (Nirtan)

This is another song inspired by the magnificent landscape of the O'Hara Sufi camp experience. It uses some well known Sufi sacred phrases: *Ya Fatah* (pronounced ya fah-tah), a *wazifa* or one of the 99 Beautiful Names of God mentioned in the Koran, each invoking one of the attributes of the Divine (*Ya Fatah* invites that Divine quality which opens the way before us); and *Al Hum dul' illah* (pronounced all-hum-dool-ill-lah, with emphasis on the 'hum' syllable), meaning all praise to the Divine Being.

OH THE BEAUTY

Words and Music by C.A.Sokoloff

Oh The Be-au-ty Oh The Won-der Oh The Bles-sing Of It All Oh The Fee-ling Oh The Won-der Oh The Bles-sing Of It All Ya Fa-tah Ya Fa-tah Al Hum Dul Il-lah Al Hum Dul Il--lah Ya Fa-tah Ya Fa-tah Al Hum Dul Il-lah Al Hum Dul Il-lah

Oh, the Beauty

LYRICS:

1. Oh, the beauty,
2. Oh, the wonder,
3. Oh, the blessing
4. of it all.
5. Oh, the feeling,
6. Oh, the wonder,
7. Oh, the blessing
8. of it all.
9. Ya Fatah, Ya Fatah
10. Al hum dul' illah, Al hum dul' illah (repeat 9 & 10)

MOVEMENTS:

Before You Begin: Standing in circle, find a partner (see partner dance instructions, p.34)

1. Starting in a circle, holding hands, move to right, walking in line of direction

2. facing circle, step backwards, to a slight bow (humbling bow to the wonder of being)

3. walk into centre of circle, raising arms in exaltation

4. Spin out back to place.

5. Repeat 1   6. Repeat 2   7. Repeat 3   8. Repeat 4

9. Face partner and gesture, palms held to heart and opening to partner, walk around each other with this gesture

10. Coming back to place, spin and progress by walking to next partner. Repeat. After second partner, spin and progress to greet new partner, but return to circle and back to 1.

Chanuka, Chanuka

Music & words by C.A. Sokoloff (Nirtan)

The Jewish celebration of Chanuka, the Festival of Lights, has always been one of my favourites. Like many Jewish holidays, Chanuka is a celebration of the ideal of spiritual liberty, the very same ideal at the basis of Hazrat Inayat Khan's Sufi Message. Chanuka, meaning rededication, also affirms a return to the light and spirit after a period of darkness. It no doubt has origins in very early agrarian Solstice rituals. The story of Chanuka relates how the Jews were forbidden to practise their religion, their Holy Temple in Jerusalem defiled and its Eternal Light of God extinguished; and how a handful of resistors miraculously drove away an oppressive and mighty regime and returned to rededicate their temple. However, the temple's Eternal Light, symbolic of the undying Light of God, could only be kindled with Holy Oil and after a great search, only enough Holy Oil for a single night could be found (and eight full days before more could be produced). Chanuka is celebrated by lighting candles, one more each night, every night for eight days. This symbolizes the miracle that, during the rededication of the temple, a tiny vial of oil, only enough for a single night, through prayer and faith, burned continuously for eight days until new Holy Oil could be made, so that the Light of God, would never again be extinguished. I remember the late Rabbi Shlomo Carlebach (blessed be He) saying, "Chanuka is the time of year when we start all over again. When you start again, you don't have very much, just a little. But you pray, please God let this little light of mine last forever." The lighting of the Chanuka candles also symbolizes the return from the darkest time of year, with the light of the candles, more each night, reflecting the coming of the light, more each day. This song and dance is particularly suited to sharing with children. Children especially will enjoy celebrating Chanuka and taking turns lighting the Chanuka candles.

Chanuka, Chanuka

LYRICS:
1. Chanuka, Chanuka, candles burning bright.
2. Little candles: one, two, three, four (2nd time: five, six, seven, eight)
   Let your light fill the night.
3. Where there is darkness, let there be light;
4. Where there is fear, let freedom reign,
5. And as of old let a miracle occur,
   Let there be peace on earth. (repeat 4 times)

MOVEMENTS:
Before You Begin: Stand in circle and find a partner (follow General Instructions for partner dances, p. 34)

1. Holding hands in circle use modified grapevine step to move to the right (step to right, cross left foot in front, step to right, cross left foot behind)—2 full grapevine sets (on last step of 2nd grapevine set lift right foot, preparing to reverse direction)

2. Circle reverses direction with same step only done in reverse, (right foot crosses in front, step to left, right foot crosses behind, step to left)

3. Take four steps in to centre of circle, raise arms, and release hands and clap on 'light'

4. spin out

5. Grand chain: face partner and offer right hand, walk past them to next partner and offer left hand, repeat

To End: Repeat the 'Let there be peace' chorus and Grand chain an extra chorus as desired. Slow tempo on last repetition, everyone stand in circle, hands joined and arms held high and then finish with a spin.

CHANUKA , CHANUKA

By C.A. Sokoloff

© Copyright 1981

Next Year In Jeruselum
(Passover Dance)
Music & words by C.A. Sokoloff (Nirtan)

Passover is another Jewish holiday which celebrates spiritual liberty. A celebration of early Spring, Passover marks the exodus of the Hebrews from Egypt, freedom from bondage and slavery; rebirth and renewal. In the broader sense we can use this holiday to remind ourselves that we have been enslaved, often by our own preconceived ideas; subject to limitations, many of them self-imposed. The first two nights of Passover or *Pesach* as it is known in Hebrew, a ritual dinner called the *seder* is held, in which the prayer "Next year in Jerusalem" is spoken. This is the metaphoric 'Jerusalem,' city of peace and spiritual awakening. This dance has a joyous chorus which can enliven a dance meeting.

NEXT YEAR IN JERUSALEM

By C.A. Sokoloff

May The Liv- ing Heart Soar On

Wings Of Spi- ri- tu- al Free- dom, For Cap- tive No

More, We Cast Off Li- mi- ta- tion. Free We Are,

Free To Be, Free To Raise Our Fa- mi- lies, Free To Speak,

Free To Say, Free To Sing And Free To Pray---

(fast)

Next Year In Je- ru- sa- lem, Next Year In Je- ru- sa- lem

Next Year in Jerusalem

LYRICS:
1. May the living heart soar on wings of spiritual freedom,
   For captive no more we cast off limitation.
2. Free we are, free to be, free to raise our families,
3. Free to speak, free to say, free to sing and free to pray...
4. Next year in Jerusalem, next year in Jerusalem,
5. Next year in Jerusalem, next year in Jerusalem.

MOVEMENTS:
1. Stand in circle holding hands. Begin a modified grapevine step to the right (step right, left foot crosses in front, step right, left foot crosses behind). Continue in this fashion.

2. Facing in to circle, on each phrase beginning 'free' do part of a series of steps, appropriately called Jacob's Ladder, which form a box shape. First the right foot moves right (on 'free we')and left foot steps together (on 'are'); on next 'free to..' right foot moves forward to centre of circle and left foot steps together; on following 'free to..' step to left and right foot follows, and on fourth 'free to...' left foot takes a step back and right foot follows. In short form the Box step pattern is: step right, left together; right foot forward, left together; step left, right together; left foot back, right together.

3. Repeat Jacob's Ladder step described in 2.

4. Hold hands, tempo picks up and circle begins to run in quick, small steps.

5. Reverse directions and continue.

Face centre for 1.

Part Four

A Musical Universal Worship

To Hazrat Pir-o-Murshid Inayat Khan and his early students or *mureeds* we owe the deeply moving Universal Worship Service, in which the great religious traditions of the world are celebrated on a single altar. In this service Pir-o-Murshid Inayat Khan's teaching of "the essential unity of religious ideals" is clearly demonstrated through the lighting of candles for each religion from a single candle representing the Divine Light of God, and through the reading of sacred texts on a single theme from the scripture of each religion. The Universal Worship service can be a tremendous vehicle for bringing people together in harmony, tolerance and understanding. I was inspired to create music for parts of this service after reading the biography of dancer Ruth St. Denis, an innovator in the art of modern dance, who has been called the Mother of the Dances of Universal Peace. St. Denis considered all dance to be worship and wished to create a Mass service which would be entirely danced. This idea led to the thought that, set to music, the Universal Worship Service could be performed as a Divine Opera, in which all parts of service could be sung and danced, including the scripture readings, as almost all sacred scriptures of the world are intended to be sung in their original languages. With this concept as inspiration, the melodies for various parts of the service soon manifested, although the performance as Sacred Opera, has not yet taken place. Still, in our community services, many prefer to use the musical settings which lend a heart quality and devotional beauty to the service. I have reproduced here the music for the major parts of the service. While the prayers Saum and Salat have also been set to music, they are quite complex and perhaps best suited to a solo vocalist, hence not included in this volume.

While striving always in this service to present each of the religions mentioned with, as Pir Hidayat Inayat-Khan stresses, "as much reverence and dignity as is felt by its adherents," there can also be room for flexibility and growth to make the Universal Worship a living, meaningful ritual. I remember Murshid Shamcher Bryn Beorse, who was one of the original mureeds of Hazrat Pir-o-Murshid Inayat Khan, relating that Pir-o-Murshid Inayat Khan said "the Universal Worship is to be done in any way that is appropriate." At the Lake

O'Hara Sufi camp Siraj David Murray has developed a marvellous Living Altar ceremony, in which dozens of people are involved, in recent years making use of the musical settings here offered. In our local services, in addition to this music, we sometimes chant together from each of the traditions before the scripture reading. There have also been special occasions such as a July 5 dance meeting (the birthday of Hazrat Inayat Khan) in which we have substituted a dance instead of a scripture reading for each of the religions. It is also possible to use the musical settings for the various parts of the service as the music for a dance which embodies the meaning of the words (ie. "To the glory..." or "We offer....") This can be a deeply moving experience. Rather than suggest choreographed movements for such dances, I believe individuals and groups may find the personal exploration of how these sentiments might be embodied through dance to be a most valuable experience. I would be very interested to hear of any such experiments. It should be noted that, while it is not included here, there exists music and movements for the final blessing, and this blessing dance is often used at a conclusion of the Universal Worship Service. Please note that the references to the elements of the Universal Worship service given in the introductions to the songs, serve only to establish the context in which the segment is used, and are not meant to be taken as authoritative instruction on conducting the Universal Worship Service. Such training and ordination as a Cherag, or servant of the Universal Worship, is available through any of the Sufi organizations related to the teachings of Hazrat Inayat Khan.

Invocation
(Procession)

Music by C.A. Sokoloff (Nirtan)   *Words by Hazrat Inayat Khan*

Here is another setting of the Sufi Invocation to music. In this case, the feeling is of a gentle, quiet joy. This music can be used as the Cherags come into the room of the Universal Worship, either sung by the Cherags themselves, or by the whole assembly, or a choir, or played by one or more musicians. The song can also be used during the opening of the Service, while the Cherag is holding aloft the first candle lit.

LYRICS:
Toward the One, the Perfection of Love,
Harmony and Beauty, the Only Being,
United with All (United with All)
The Illuminated Souls,
Who form the embodiment of the Master,
The Spirit of Guidance, the Spirit of Guidance.

INVOCATION

By C.A. Sokoloff,   Words By Inayat Khan

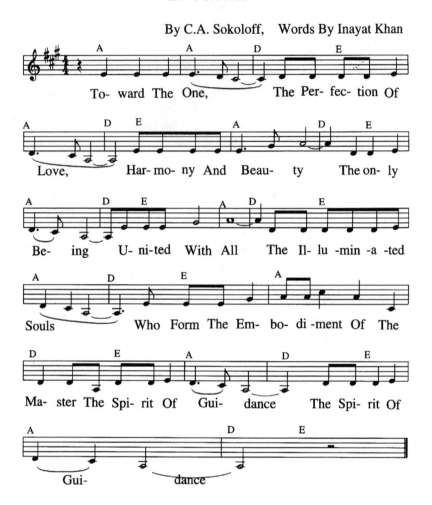

TO THE GLORY

Music by C.A. Sokoloff (Nirtan)   *Words by Hazrat Inayat Khan*

In this part of the Universal Worship service the Cherag, after lighting a taper from the high central candle representing the Divine Light, holds this taper aloft and proceeds to light the six candles arranged in a semi-circle on the altar, each representing one of the world's great religions, and a seventh candle representing "those known and unknown to the world who have held aloft the light of truth..." Before kindling each of these candles, the Cherag holds the taper high and speaks or sings the words of this song. On the words 'To the Glory..' the candle is raised in the direction of the Divine Light candle. On the words 'we kindle the light' the flame is kindled on the candle representing a religion.

LYRICS:
To the glory of the Omnipresent God we kindle the light,
symbolically representing:
1. the Hindu religion
2. the Buddhist religion
3. the Zoroastrian religion
4. the Jewish religion
5. the Christian religion
6. the religion of Islam
7. All those whether known or unknown to the world, who have held aloft the light of truth through the darkness of human ignorance.

TO THE GLORY

By C.A. Sokoloff, Words By Inayat Khan

To The Glo- ry Of The Om- ni -pre- sent

God We Kin- dle The Light Sym- bol-ic-ally

Re- pre- sent- ing The Hin- du Re- li- gion

To The Bud- dhist Re- li- gion To The

Zo- ro as- tri -an Re- li- gion To The Jew- ish

Re- li- gion To The Chris- tian Re- li- gion

To The Re- li- gion Of Is- lam To The

All Those Whe- ther Known Or Un- Known To The

World, Who Have Held A- loft The Light Of

Truth Through The Dark- ness Of Hu- man Ig- nor-

ance.

We Offer

Music by C.A. Sokoloff (Nirtan)   *Words by Hazrat Inayat Khan*

A fter the lighting of all the candles and the reciting by the assembly of the prayer 'Saum', the Cherag picks up the sacred scripture books which are placed in front of each candle and reads a selected passage on a given theme. After each reading this offering is given, with the Cherag holding the scripture on high in the direction of the Divine Light candle. After the readings from the world scriptures are concluded, and after the prayer 'Salat' has been recited, a selection from the *Gayan, Vadan, Nirtan* of Hazrat Pir-o-Murshid Inayat Khan is read, and the final offering is performed.

LYRICS:
We offer the Omniscient God
our reverence, homage and gratitude
for the light, for the light,
for the light of Thy Divine....
1. Wisdom
2. Compassion
3. Purity
4. Law
5. Self-sacrifice
6. Unity
7. Truth

WE OFFER

By C.A. Sokoloff, Words By Inayat Khan

We Of- fer The Om- ni- scient God Our

Re-ver- ence Homage And Gra- ti- tude For The Light

For The Light For The Light Of

Thy Di- vine Wis- dom We Com-pas -sion We

3rd Pu- ri- ty We 4th Law We 5th Self Sac-ri- fice We

6th U- ni- ty We Truth

THE PRAYER 'KHATUM'

Music by Nirtan (C.A. Sokoloff)   *Words by Hazrat Inayat Khan*

PRAYER, KHATUM
By C.A.Sokoloff,Words By Inayat Khan

Oh Thou Who Art The Per- fec- tion Of

Love, Har- mo- ny and Beau- ty The Lord Of

Hea- ven And Earth, O- pen Our Hearts

That We May Hear Thy Voice Which Con- stant-

ly Com- eth From With- in Dis- close To Us

Thy Di-vine Light, Which Is Hid- den In Our

Souls That We May Know And Un- der

-stand Life Bet- ter Most Mer- ci -ful And Com-

pas- sion- ate God Give Us Thy Great Good- ness

The prayer known as 'Khatum' seems to resonate universally in the hearts of everyone who speaks or hears it. We frequently recite it at the close of our Sufi meetings, for it so well sums up the essence of Sufi thought and practice. For any who may have trouble memorizing the words of this beautiful prayer, the preceding musical setting may be of some assistance. There are one or two very slight alterations of text required to 'sing' the prayer. However, it should not be forgotten that "He or she who sings, prays twice."

LYRICS:
Oh Thou, who art the perfection of Love, Harmony and Beauty,
the Lord of Heaven and Earth;
Open our hearts that we may hear Thy voice,
which constantly cometh from within,
Disclose to us Thy Divine Light which is hidden in our souls,
that we may know and understand life better.
Most merciful and compassionate God,
give us Thy great goodness,
Teach us Thy loving forgiveness.
And raise us above the distinctions and differences,
which divide mankind.
Send us the peace of Thy Divine Spirit,
and unite us all in Thy perfect Being.
Oh, send us the peace of Thy Divine Spirit,
and unite us all in Thy perfect Being.